ABOUT THE

Shirley Toulson is a poet, educationist, and author of many books including *Celtic Journeys* (Hutchinson), *The Drovers' Roads of Wales, East Anglia: walking the ley lines and ancient tracks; Derbyshire: Exploring the ancient tracks and mysteries of Mercia* (Whittet Books); *Moors of the South West: I & II* (Hutchinson).

Eagle of St. John with halo and crosses. Gospel of St. Matthew.
Book of Kells. (*from The Celtic Design Coloring Book,
Dover Publications Inc.*)

THE CELTIC ALTERNATIVE

The Christianity We Lost

Shirley Toulson

RIDER

LONDON SYDNEY AUCKLAND JOHANNESBURG

Copyright © Shirley Toulson 1987

First published in 1987 by Rider
Reprinted 1990
This edition published in 1992 by Rider
An imprint of Random Century Group Ltd,
20 Vauxhall Bridge Road, London SW1V 2SA

Random Century Group Australia (Pty) Ltd
20 Alfred Street, Milsons Point,
Sydney, NSW 2061, Australia

Random Century New Zealand Ltd
18 Poland Road, Glenfield
Auckland 10, New Zealand

Random Century Group South Africa (Pty) Ltd
PO Box 337, Bergvlei 2012, South Africa

Printed and bound in Great Britain by
The Guernsey Press Co. Ltd., Guernsey, Channel Islands

The right of Shirley Toulson to be identified
as the author of this work has been asserted
by her in accordance with
Copyright, Designs and Patents Act, 1988.

A catalogue record for this book is available
from the British Library.

ISBN 0-7126-1478-8

This book is printed on recycled paper.

Contents

Acknowledgements

I am grateful to the Benedictine Community at Downside Abbey, and in particular to Dom Philip Jebb and to the late Mr Joseph Collins for allowing me to use their excellent library for my researches. I should also like to thank Mother Mary Clare and her co-religionists at Fairacres, Oxford, Canon Samuel Cutt of Wells Cathedral, the Reverend Marcus Braybrooke and the Reverend Graham Jenkins of the Council of Christians and Jews, and Mr Gerald Bonner of the University of Durham's Department of Theology for their unfailing kindness in response to my requests for information and clarification. I am fully aware that these people are unlikely to be in sympathy with many of my conclusions. That only increases my gratitude.

The quotations from the Bible are all taken from the King James Authorized Version and, unless otherwise stated, those from contemporary writings come from Bede's *Ecclesiastica Brittanica*. I have used the translation made by Leo Sherley-Price (Penguin Books, 1955).

Prologue

In the so-called Dark Ages a religion flourished in the islands of Britain which had more in common with Buddhism than with the institutional Christianity of the West. It was based on a church founded without martyrs, and one that neither inflicted suffering nor encouraged bitter theological disputes. It was marked by compassion and moderation in all its dealings. Above all, it was a religion of country people, for after the legions withdrew from the Roman garrisons there were no towns in Britain, and it was practised in tribal groups, by people who had previously worshipped their own local deities through the rituals prescribed by the druids, who formed their priestly caste. When news of Christianity first came to Ireland and mainland Britain, the new faith was smoothly grafted onto the old.

This was made possible because so many of the tenets of both faiths were the same. The druids, for example, encouraged an unshakable belief in the continuity of life after physical death. Many druidic practices were equally acceptable to Christians, and in particular the custom of the 'soul friend' (called *periglour* in Wales, *anmchara* in Ireland). He was a person who acted as spiritual guide and counsellor to young monks and to new converts. He took the part of confessor, but would offer only wisdom, advice and encouragement to his juniors, refraining from taking on the power to grant absolution for any sins. In that the Celtic Church followed the practice of the Celtic druids, who communed with the gods without themselves adopting divine authority.

Such an attitude left each person free, with an independence that was to become a thorn in the flesh of the continental establishment and so contribute to the eventual downfall of the Celtic Church. For the papal authorities in Rome, like the leaders of the Roman Empire before them, demanded control over all aspects of a man's soul. 'Who cannot but condemn the insolent and impious assertion that man can live without sin of his own free will?' was the rhetorical question posed by Pope John in a letter written in 634 to the Irish Scots denouncing their independence from Rome. John found it 'blaspehemous folly' for any person to imagine that he could work out his own salvation and was particularly incensed at the peculiarly British heresy of pelagianism, which denied the existence of original sin and declared that a man could further the work of Grace by his own willpower. No wonder the authorities in Rome found such a doctrine dangerous. In order to uphold the central authority of the Church it was imperative to encourage a faith dependent on a grace which only the leaders of the Church could interpret. To suggest anything else was a serious undermining of papal authority. Envoys were sent from Rome to Britain to counter this heresy, and to baptize people into the Church of Rome.

These new converts, like the Romano-British Christians of earlier centuries (such as Patrick, who took his faith to Ireland, where a form of Celtic Christianity was already flourishing), shaved their head with a central tonsure when they took holy orders. The Celtic monks, on the other hand, retained the druidic tonsure and shaved the front of their heads from ear to ear. It was a badge of difference, a slight matter to our eyes, which was to be blown up into one of the main causes of dissension when the Roman and Celtic Churches came to a confrontation in the mid-seventh century.

A more drastic divergence, however, and one that caused more practical difficulties, was the discrepancy over the calculation for the date of Easter. The Celtic Church was initially in phase with Rome on this matter, reckoning the anniversary of the Resurrection on an eighty-four-year cycle. Indeed, three British bishops were present at the Council of Arles in 314 and presumably assented to the doctrine proclaimed there that Easter be celebrated *Uno die et una tempore per omnem orbem.* However, when, in 458, the Roman Church adopted a calendar based on a nineteen-year cycle, the Celtic Church saw no reason to change its own practices. By that time the difference in date might have become symbolic, and would have strengthened the resolve of the leaders of the Celtic Church to keep the feast at the same time that their fathers would have done.

For the main point at issue between the two Churches was power and the administration of power. For the Celts, the bishops (including the Bishop of Rome) were valuable executive officials, but as such they did not have the spiritual authority that was invested in the abbots, many of whom presided over institutions which they had founded themselves, and who gathered disciples and converts around them. It was a dispensation fitting to rural communities, who expected to conduct their affairs in small groups and in comparative isolation. But it was intolerable to a quasi-military power which needed to control its institutions through an inflexible network of communications.

By 604, when Laurentius had succeeded Augustine at Canterbury, there was such bitterness between the Roman and the Celtic Christians that the new primate complained than when the Irish bishop Dagan visited him 'he not only refused to eat with us, but even to take his meal in the same house as ourselves.' The differences came to a head during the Lent of 664, a year in which the Roman Easter fell on 21 April, and the contest focused on Northumbria, where the monks of the abbey of Lindisfarne, which had been founded by Aidan of Iona, were all loyal adherents of the Celtic Church. On Aidan's death Finan the new abbot of Lindisfarne, was confronted by Ronan, an Irish monk who had studied in Gaul and Italy, and who was determined to establish the Roman Easter and all that went with it. The split that this occasioned in the abbey of Lindisfarne paralleled a split in the royal court, where the Anglian king Oswy followed the tradition of the Celtic Church, while his Kentish wife Eanfleda and her chaplain Romanus were loyal to the Roman practices and the rites of Canterbury.

Their final confrontation took place at Whitby (then known by its Anglian name of Streaneshalch), a double monastery ruled over by the Abbess Hilda, sister of the queen of the East Angles and a woman much admired and respected by Aidan of Lindisfarne. The specific points at issue were the style of the tonsure, the discrepancies over the calculations of the date of Easter, the persistence of the Pelagian heresy, and the reluctance of the leaders of the Celtic Church to undertake any missionary work among the hordes of invading Saxons.

A more fundamental difference arose out of the conflicting approaches to the life of the spirit, indicated by the discrepancies between John's message of love and the authority of Peter, nominated by Christ as founder of his Church and keeper of the Keys of Heaven. The leaders of the Celtic Church had a particularly strong devotion to John's Gospel. That is made clear in the life of Columba, and in the fact that when Boisil, the Irish abbot of Melrose, was dying, the young Cuthbert read passages from that Gospel to him every day at his request. The affection which the Celtic Church had for the words of John was explicitly stated during the discourse at Whitby, which was recorded, apparently verbatim, by Bede.

On that occasion Peter conquered through fear, for when he was assured that that apostle alone held the Keys to Heaven, King Oswy, who had the ultimate responsibility of choosing between the two Churches, declared that he would not dare to alienate the saint who had the power of leading him to bliss. 'This is the door-keeper, whom I will not contradict, but will, as far as I know and am able in all things obey his decrees, lest perchance, when I come to the gates of the kingdom of heaven, there should be none to open them, he being my adversary who is proved to have the keys.'

It seems either a somewhat cynical or else a pathetically cowardly and pragmatic ending to a discourse carried out with the utmost fervour by Colman, then abbot of Lindisfarne, who had to speak through the Saxon Cedd, who acted as interpreter for both the Celtic and the Roman Churches. Colman pleaded desperately for the continuance of the Church to which he belonged; while his fellow North Countryman, the urbane Wilfrid, who acted as spokesman for the Frankish Agilbert, a former bishop of Dorchester-on-Thames, who had no English, put forward the case for Roman domination.

Wilfrid had received his education at Lindisfarne, having entered the monastery at the age of fourteen. However, he never took the Celtic tonsure, and before he was twenty, 'being a shrewd young man', as Bede wrote, 'he gradually came to realize that the way of life taught by the Scots was very imperfect.' So he decided to visit Rome, an ambition which he achieved with the help of Queen Eanfleda. On his return journey he took the tonsure in the Roman form at Lyons; and when he got back to Northumbria he was ordained by Agilbert himself, according to the Roman rites. Even his latter-day admirers of the nineteenth and twentieth centuries

have to admit that he was an overbearing man, infected
with the Roman love of power and display. It was he who
engineered the outcome of Whitby and who was the true
victor of the debate. His concluding speech, as Bede
recounts it, was rude, patronizing and hurtful to the
Church which had nourished him. In words which surely
belong more to his own pride than to the wit of Agilbert
he declared that he did not deny that Columba and his
followers were 'true servants of God and that they loved
Him in primitive simplicity,' but he then roughly
inquired of Colman and his followers; 'Although your
Fathers were holy men, do you imagine that they, a few
men in a corner of a remote island, are to be preferred
before the universal church of Christ throughout the
world?'

Colman, who had come to Lindisfarne from Iona at
the death of Finan only three years before the Synod was
held, and who had always been highly regarded by Oswy
for his kindly prudence, found himself unable to accept
the outcome of Wilfrid's debating. Taking thirty of his
monks with him, he left Lindisfarne for Iona, and from
there went west to Ireland, founding his own monastery
at Inishbofin in County Galway. Lindisfarne was left in
the hands of Tuda, a man from southern Ireland, where
the Roman customs as taught by Patrick were practised.
Colman was unhappy at the arrangement, and Oswy
conceded to his request that the gentle Eata, a former
pupil of Aidan and at that time prior of Melrose, should
come back to look after the monks who had remained in
Northumbria.

As for Wilfrid, he went on to a life of ecclesiastical
splendour and, finding no prelate worthy of the task in
England, demanded to be consecrated by twelve
Frankish bishops in Compiègne. Thereafter he gave a
great deal of his energies to raising money in order to
glorify the abbey of Hexam, whose church, together
with its monastic buildings, was to become the richest

ecclesiastical settlement north of the Alps. It remained so at least until the twelfth century, when William of Malmesbury claimed that those who visited Hexam 'had before their eyes a model of Roman magnificence'. In the seventh century it must have made a staggering contrast to the modest timber-built, thatched church at Lindisfarne which Colman's predecessor, Finan, had caused to be built there.

Colman was not alone in his stand against Roman domination. Not until fifty years after the decision at Whitby did the Pictish Christians of northeast Scotland begin to desert the teachings of the Celtic Church as they had been brought to them by Columba. The monks of Iona reluctantly adopted the Roman Easter at about the same time. In Wales, however, the Celtic Church retained its independence for a hundred years, and the Cornish persisted in following Celtic rites until the tenth century. It could be that those areas were encouraged in their dissidence by the calamities that fell upon England soon after the decision at Whitby was made known. Probably about a month later (the actual date of the Synod is uncertain), at 10 o'clock in the morning of 3 May, there was an eclipse of the sun. It was followed by a plague which struck the south of England and then spread to Northumbria, where Tuda was one of its victims.

Cedd, who had acted as interpreter at Whitby, died of the plague at Lastingham in Yorkshire on 26 October of that year. The disaster persisted and crossed the water. The Irish annals report that many synods were held on the subject of abandoning the Celtic tonsure and the method of calculating Easter, and that the matter was so bitterly disputed that 'many evils resulted in Ireland in consequence of this; and also a great murrain of cows, and a very great famine, and many diseases, and the devastation of Ireland by foreign hordes.' That makes it clear that all these disasters were interpreted as an unhappy comment on the outcome at Whitby.

Most of our knowledge about all these events comes from the pen of Bede, a monk of Jarrow, who compiled a history of the English Church and its people, which he completed in 731, four years before his own death. Although he was a loyal adherent of the Catholic Church of Rome, he had a great affection and reverence for the humility of the leaders of the Celtic Church and, like them, held the Gospel of John particularly close to his heart. He was actually working on an Anglo-Saxon translation from it at the time of his death.

In the earlier sections of his work Bede drew on the writings of the sixth-century Gildas, a monk from Llaniltud in Wales, who ended his days as an abbot in Brittany. Gildas, who chastized the British clerics for their decadence, blamed their behaviour for the fact that the country was being overrun by the Saxon pagans. He had been born in 495, the year of the battle of Mount Bladon, in which the invading Saxon forces had been temporarily defeated and confined to the south and east of the country. There they followed their own pagan religion, which, as it sprang from the same Indo-European roots, had similarities with that practised by the Celtic druids.

Our own ideas about the Anglo-Saxons have become set in a fixed pattern which does not always reflect the true reality. It has been suggested that we would come nearer the truth if we could think of them as Celtic-Saxons, and, as far as religious affinities go, that would be more accurate. Many of the leading members of the Irish/Scottish Celtic Church in Iona and Lindisfarne bear Saxon names such as Cuthbert and Chad, and were probably descendants of those Saxons who were initially invited to the Northeast by the Romans in order to help them quell the invading hordes of Picts and Scots who were making the country untenable by the legions. By the time that the Romans had completely withdrawn, the

Saxons had intermarried with the Britons and settled down to farm the new lands. The violent pirate invaders, forerunners of the Viking raiders, which the native Britons had to contend with during the fifth and sixth centuries were another matter.

Nevertheless, they were the English – not Angles but angels – whose pagan beauty so won the heart of Pope Gregory the Great when he saw them offered as slaves in the Roman marketplace. Slavery itself was not felt to be objectionable at that time. If Christians raised their voices against it, as Patrick did, it was not against the institution itself but against the spiritual dangers that could befall a Christian sold into a heathen household. So whoever was selling the English boys in Rome was not chastized. The point was that they came from a corner of a Christian country which had been deliberately left heathen by the surrounding clergy. So in 597, the year of Columba's death, Gregory, a great authoritarian, who had burned books in the Palatine Library lest they should encourage dissent and heresy, sent his advocate Augustine to Britain. He landed somewhere on the Isle of Thanet; scholars still dispute the exact location, although a nineteenth-century Warden of the Cinque Ports had a great cross raised just outside Ramsgate, to mark the supposed spot. Wherever he landed, he was soon to make his headquarters at Canterbury.

For the next half century, the evangelizing Church of Rome and the ministering Celts lived uneasily side by side, celebrating Easter at times which could be as much as a month apart. When matters came to a head at Whitby and the Celtic Church ceased to exist, we lost a form of individual Christianity which, through its druidic roots, was truly linked to the perennial philosophy of humanity. It is possible that the battle of words which was waged in 644 was even more of a turning point in the history of these islands than the battle fought out by contending armies at Hastings in 1066.

The leaders of the Celtic Church were called saints – few of them have actually been canonized; the term was used widely – in the sense that Paul used it in referring to his fellow Christians. In Britain the term also meant 'revered' or 'learned'; and as education was in the hands of the Church the term 'saint' came to imply anybody who could read and write. Because we have come to associate the term purely with those men and women who have been nominated by the Catholic Church at Rome for evincing some miraculous, supernatural intervention in the course of their earthly existence, I have dropped the title completely in this book, in so far as it refers to any particular individual. I do that partly out of the spirit that inspires the Quakers to seek 'that of God in every man' and so by implication to find no man more peculiarly divine than his fellows; and partly to avoid the confusion that the use of the term brings about and the sickly odour of sanctity that goes with it. If the Celtic use of the word 'saint' were to be translated into Hebrew terminology, it would appear as *rabbi* (teacher) or *abba* (father).

The leaders of the Church we have lost acted as teachers and parents to their followers; above all, they were men and women beloved for their charity, patience and quiet good sense. They lived in troubled times when pestilence and plague were rife, and when famine was so acute that in the 440s people in England were actually fighting each other for food. Yet the Christian 'saints' remained faithful to the golden rule of Christ's love, and were convincingly close to both the unseen world of spiritual truths and to the material density of the earth and her creatures. Above all, they followed out the injunction of Micah, 'to do justly, and to love mercy and to walk humbly with thy God.' They were people of great humility. The advisers of kings, they forbore to ride horses when they went on their journeys lest they lost touch with the common people. They followed a religion that was primarily concerned with the relations between people, a religion of an isolated rural landscape, in which to meet a fellow human being is to hail him.

At Whitby we traded that for a city-based religion, and in the cities people are amassed in crowds, to be manipulated, no matter how benevolently. Now that we are realizing the deadly dangers of our mass techno-logical society, it is time, I think, to turn back and con-sider the humanity of the men and women of the Celtic Church. Their Church could have been our inheritance – as it is, we can still visit the places associated with it, look at some of the things that were made by its adherents, and catch something of the spirit of its leaders in the descendants of the people who were their friends.

PART ONE

The Sources

— 1 —

The Druids

All religion is to do with light, even if it is not directly concerned with sun worship. Beyond the symbolism lies an actuality that is especially relevant to Britain and Ireland. These islands are oddly placed. We enjoy the long summer days and endure the equally long winter nights of a northern latitude, while having the benefit of the fairly temperate climate which the Gulf Stream brings us. Indeed, it seems that in the last two millenia BC the climate was even milder than the one we experience now, so that upland wastes, such as Dartmoor, could be farmed extensively. I should like to bear all this in mind as I discuss the druidic religion on which the Celtic Church was founded, and speculate on the unknown beliefs which motivated the Stone and Bronze Age people as they built their carefully ornamented barrows and megalithic henges.

I shall begin in Ireland, in the fertile valley of the Boyne to the north of Dublin, and the partly excavated and restored barrow of New Grange. Its curved passageway leads into a domed chamber whose corbelled roof had withstood the weathers of 5000 years, and whose stones are covered in careful spiral designs, diagonal patterns, chevrons and triangles.

It is a wonder at any time on the year, but in a clear winter dawn, when the rays of the sunrise at the solstice

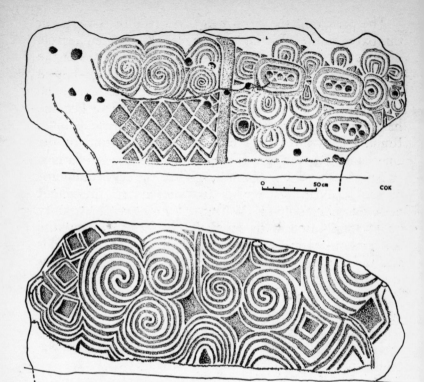

Reproduced (*by permission of Mrs Claire O'Kelly and Hickey & Byrne, Cork*)

New Grange Stones

are directed through the little window above the entrance to make a glowing carpet for the chamber, the natural phenomenon is raised to a mystical level. The sun brings light to the chamber of the dead, for it was to this place that the living brought the bones of the people cremated by the riverside. The light is more than a symbol of hope; it transcends mortality.

The people of the Bronze Age realized the sanctity of this barrow, built by the 'old people' and erected a circle of tall stones to protect it. Through the wizardry of the smiths, men learned the use of iron. The tall, fair-haired Celts from Central and Eastern Europe discovered the rich lands of the Boyne, and for them the barrow became the home of the *sidhe*, the fairy folk or little people. Round the winter fires heroic tales were told of the Tuatha de Danaan, the divine children of the All Father.

Among them was Mannon, god of the sea, conductor of the souls in the world after death and messenger between men and gods. With the coming of Christianity he became fused with Michael the Archangel, whose September feast comes at a time when the light holds steady for the autumnal equinox, and whose dedications are still to be found on hilltops and headlands throughout Britain. Moreover the dragon-slaying Archangel, upholder of courage and truth (the two essential virtues of the unblemished Celtic kings), remains an inspiration for seekers after wisdom both within and without the established Church.

Nearly all the medieval hilltop St Michael churches (some of which, like St Michael of the Rock on Brentor on the western edge of Dartmoor, are still in use) stand on sites which were familiar holy ground to the men of the Iron Age villages. It is significant that in Devon and Cornwall, where the Celtic Church maintained its practices until the tenth century, the cult of Michael was strongest. Even now the Michael dedications are more numerous in those counties than in any other region of Britain.

A little farther east, across the inland sea of Somerset, the Iron Age people who lived in the swampy lake villages brought their dead for burial to the slopes of the limestone outcrop that forms Glastonbury Tor. It has been a sacred place for millenia, and a constant stream of people still climb up to the remaining tower of the last St

Michael church to stand there. It was destroyed by an earthquake in the fourteenth century. In a field below the Tor's summit there are two venerable oaks which are believed to owe their existence to the grove in which the druidic priests of Glastonbury performed their mysteries.

Druidism was a priestly caste rather than a religion. There are disputes about the origin of the word, which some scholars find to be derived from the Vedic *vid*, 'to know', and which others link with the Greek *drus*, 'an oak'. Both explanations are appealing. The first emphasizes the Indo-European origin of the cult; the second accentuates the ritual association with trees, emphasized by both classical writers and the tellers of folk tales. For it was not only the oak that the druids held sacred; they are also said to have made ritual uses of the rowan and the yew. The former has long been held as a tree that will ward off evil spirits. The latter had a more particular purpose. On the wood of yew trees the druids are thought to have inscribed powerful words in their linear Ogham script, although the only Ogham that has come down to us is carved on stone, usually alongside Latin letters.

Nevertheless it is with the Druids that we come to history and the written word in Britain. Although they never transmitted the mysteries of their religion to writing, preferring to perfect an oral tradition which took students twenty years in their colleges to memorize, they knew both Latin and Greek. They were the only educators. They took a few well-born girls as well as noble young men into their schools, and they included both men and women in their ranks. However, most of our knowledge about them comes from their enemies. Although Caesar claimed the druid Diviciacus among his friends, he had no scruples in exaggerating the barbarity of the enemies of Rome. Yet he had to admit the learning, courage and the moral integrity which they showed in performing the rites of their faith and in conducting the affairs of state, for the druids could be decision makers in public matters, acting as counsellors to kings and tribal leaders. Moreover, it is from Caesar that we learn that the Gauls sent their young men to the druidic colleges in Britain. Later we shall see how these colleges became the monastic schools of the sixth and seventh centuries.

Any organized religion produces a hierarchy. Among the Celtic tribes the druids, as shamans, priests and administrators, corresponded in caste to the Indian Brahmin; below them came the *filid* – bards, poets and seers; and the third rank was reserved for princelings and warriors. On mainland Britain the legions could easily work with such an ordered society, even if they were confused and mistrustful of the absence of shrines and sacred buildings. In Ireland, where the Romans never came, the matter was never put to the test. In that country the first confrontation the druids had to face came with Christianity, a faith that some of them had already predicted.

Even that confrontation was not the complete overthrow of one regime by another. The Christian priests and monks of the Celtic Church adopted the druidic tonsure, which shaved the front of the head from ear to ear; they wore the same white robes and carried a similar staff or crook. In the legends they even engaged with the druids in contests of wizardry, an enthralling imaginative reconstruction of the disputes that certainly went on in fact. So the hagiographers tell us that when Columba journeyed across Scotland to confront the Pictish king Brude, from whom he hoped to attain full legal rights to Iona, he had to prove his worth in a battle of miracles against the court druid. Their contests involved raising storms on Loch Ness and using floating stones to cure the sick. Columba eventually confirmed the supremacy of the power that worked through him when he restored a dead slavegirl to life.

Yet in symbolic terms Columba found it no sacrilege to refer to Christ as his druid in one of his many hymns; and the druids retained their status as wise men and counsellors well into the Christian era. Two things made it easier for the new religion to absorb rather than to defeat the old. The first was the firm Celtic belief in an afterlife which could take the intermediary form of reincarnation; the second was the druidic pattern of 'soul friends'. In such a capacity a druid acted as a spiritual guide and earthly counsellor, but not as a confessor with powers of absolution. This role of soul friends was subsequently adopted by the Christian abbots of the Celtic settlements and the same term was used.

Because the druids had set the pattern, Christian priests were often involved, albeit uneasily, in affairs of state; and some of the druids seem to have retained their civic positions in regional Christian courts. In the legends the Christian King Arthur is always linked with Merlin, wizard, madman and druid, who is supposed to have met his death in the late sixth century after a fatal meeting with Kentigern (Glasgow's Mungo) in the hills above Moffat.

As Merlin is also supposed to be buried in Brittany, besides several other places, the stories about him obviously lie in fable, but their origin stands on historical fact. We come nearer to history in the accounts of the druids of Tara, where the kings of Ireland were elected and confirmed in their office. Among warring tribes, in an age when untamed nature gave man a tenuous hold on life, it would have been impractical to have adopted a system of inheritance by primogeniture. Instead, the most able man, in terms of personality and physique, was chosen as ruler. The part played by the druids in that selection was inevitably taken over by the Church, but the transition did not run smoothly. Columba had to claim angelic intervention to support his choice of king for Dalraida in western Scotland; and Patrick, distressed that the Irish kings continued the pagan practice of marrying the land in the form of a symbolic union with a white mare representing the goddess Epona, was forced into an open confrontation, on the sacred hill of Tara, with the two chief druids of King Laogaire. According to legend, when one of these magicians cursed the Christian faith, Patrick prayed for his destruction, and immediately the scoffer was raised into the air to such a height that when he fell he shattered his skull against a stone. This so incensed the king that he tried to seize Patrick and his followers. His efforts were in vain. In response to the saint's prayers Tara became shrouded in a heavy mist and an earthquake caused all its palaces and ceremonial halls to shudder. Finally Patrick and his followers eluded their pursuers by being transformed into a herd of deer. Both these miracles were druidic in origin, for the druids were supposed to have the power to call up a mist at will, and as shamans they could take on animal forms.

Patrick's adventure does not seem much of a victory; and the hideous Victorian statue of the saint which broods over Tara now does little to bring Christian sanctity to the broad hill whose modest 300 feet completely dominate the plains of Meath. Nor is the place claimed for the old gods by the much more acceptable figure of Cernunnos inscribed on a standing stone in the churchyard. The truth lies in the tension between old and new; in the barrow, which, like its greater contemporary at New Grange, contains stones decorated with the swirling patterns which were eventually to find a place in Celtic manuscript art, and in the earthworks which mark the great halls where Patrick and his followers had their real disputes with the druids, and where Columba's seafaring kinsman, Niall of the Nine Hostages, ruled in the fifth century.

The Church had to learn how to accept its inheritance from the pre-Christian era. Among the druidic inheritance was a culture culled from the ancient beliefs of the

The Sources

Indo-European stock from which the majority of the Celts originated, but they were not the only influence on the emerging Church. As well as the tall, fair-haired Celtic people, there was a race of small, dark Celts, whose language (as nineteenth-century scholars were already noting) carried traces of Berber roots. These Semetic people, reaching Ireland from the southern shores of the Mediterranean, belonged to a trading, seafaring people whose kingdom was the Atlantic seaboard of Europe.

In fable and legend we hear of the people who came to Ireland, travelling through Spain as they journeyed from Egypt, Sicily and Crete. In fact archaeologists have discovered sufficient artefacts to prove that there was a lively trade along this route. A trade in goods goes along with a trade in ideas, and so prepared the way for the Coptic influence, which was to produce a church that was nearer Byzantium than Rome in outlook, and which is remembered today more in the Orthodox than in the Roman Catholic tradition.

It is possible that the Irish druids first heard of Christianity from an Egyptian or Jewish source. Certainly Patrick was not the first with the gospel. Back in the third century, Origen, writing in Alexandria, had claimed that parts of Britain inaccesible to Rome had been subjected to Christ. He was clearly referring to Ireland and the northwest of Scotland, where the legions never penetrated, and to Wales, Cornwall and Brigantia (a stretch of northern England), which came late under Roman control. When the young Patrick, the son of a solid Romano-British family living south of the Solway Firth, was brought across the water to Ireland as a slave, he is reported to have found Christian communities there that were already lapsing back into paganism.

At about the same time that Patrick was preaching the Trinity and confounding the resurgent pagan beliefs of the Irish, the effects of the religious tolerance expounded by the apostate caesar, Julian, were making an impact on the centres of Roman culture in Britain. On the western bank of the Severn a temple was dedicated to the Celtic hunting god, Nodens. Thousands of pilgrims were drawn to this site. Excavations which have revealed the extent of the guest house prepared for their reception testify to their numbers. The same acclaim was given to many of the other Celtic gods whom the Romans equated with their own pantheon. Sulis/Minerva, who presided over the thermal springs of Bath, and Maponus/Apollo, whose cult was marked by a stone circle at Clock-mabonstane on the Solway Firth, drew people away from the mysterious faith of a single God expressed as three persons.

Only Mannon/Michael seems to have crossed over into the new religion at its beginning, although later the triple goddess Brigid (who personified women as maiden, matron and crone) was absorbed, as we shall see, into the person of Brigid, the abbess of Kildare. It is easier to relate an incorporal archangel to a pagan god than to identify mortal men and women with local deities, although that was to happen as particular saints became identified with the spirits of hills and wells.

The cult of Michael, 'the great watcher', entered the Celtic Church through the Apocrypha of the Old Testament, and in particular through the *Book of Enoch* and the first-century *Ascension of Isaiah*. It was fitting that he should take over the pagan role of Mannon as sea god and conductor of souls in the underworld, for in Kabbalistic literature Michael is the angel set over water; and in Coptic liturgical texts of the fourth century the Archangel is referred to as the spirit which brings the souls of men into the presence of their Saviour. Indeed, as guardian and guide of the newly dead, Michael's name was incorporated into the offertory of the Roman mass for the dead until 1970.

Michael has one other aspect. In apocryphal literature

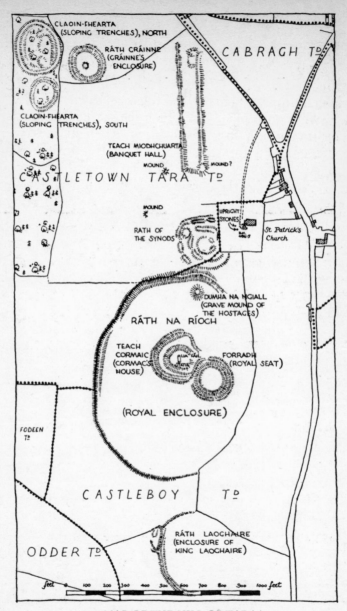

MAP OF THE HILL OF TARA

The names as given here are in accordance with the plaques marking the sites on the Hill.

(Based on the 25 inch Ordnance Survey, Co. Meath, Sheet XXXI, Plan 16, by permission of the Minister for Finance)

(Reproduced by permission of the Dundalgan Press, Dundalk, Eire) he interprets the purposes of God to Abraham, Moses and Isaiah; and when Enoch has written his volumes at the dictation of the Almighty, God tells him, 'I will give thee Enoch, My messenger, the great captain Michael, for thy writings and for the writings of thy fathers.' Many of the British hilltops on which the Archangel's dedications still stand were once places on which the sacred druidic fires were lit. In the long dark nights their flames were sometimes used for signalling as well as for worship. That gives Michael another association with communication, and I find that fitting in a tradition which, like that of the Jews, gave so much importance to prayer, regarding it less as begging than as dialogue.

The Jews

On the shores of the Dead Sea, during the time of Jesus, the Jewish sect of the Essenes practised a carefully guarded ritual dependent on a hierarchy of angels, watchers and guardians who looked after every aspect of life. When the Romans over ran the country and destroyed the temple in Jerusalem in the seventieth year of our common era, the Essenes apparently disappeared. They left no traces in the place where they had lived and worked, apart from some scrolls in sealed jars which were not discovered until the middle of the twentieth century. Although that discovery had far-reaching implications for the interpretation of the Scriptures which few people have as yet had the courage to realize, we know little of the people who conducted their lives according to the words of those scrolls.

However, we do know something of a similar group in Egypt, and it is very possible that the Essenes joined them after the dispersal. Philo, the extremely learned Jewish scholar and statesman who lived during the time of Christ, wrote about the Therapeutae, a word coined from the Greek and implying devotion to the gods as well as powers of healing. From Alexandria Philo described these people as a group of monks and nuns living in seclusion in the desert, and he wrote of them in such glowing terms that scholars have concluded that he may have been one of their number until he realized that he had no call to the contemplative life. According to the third-century historian Eusebius, Philo wrote in a similar manner of the Essenes. That fragment of his writings has been lost to us, as have at least nine of the thirty treatises which he collected together for a work called *The Allegory*, in which he argued that the literal tradition and observance of God's law, as it is expressed in the Torah, has a meaning that can only be perceived by a minority of spiritually gifted people. It was a doctrine that was to blossom into the elitism of some forms of Christian Gnosticism.

A spiritual hierarchy among men, which is one of the necessary tenets of Gnosticism or salvation by know-ledge, is quite separate from the heavenly hierarchy of the angelic host. It was the latter which was to have the greatest effect on the Celtic Church, despite the renowned scholarship of the Irish monks.

It is reasonable to presume that the Essenes' total dependence on the presence of angels, which still plays such an important part in Jewish, Catholic and Orthodox tradition, reached these islands from Egypt and North Africa, and so became built into the doctrine and practice of the Celtic Church. It is fitting that this wisdom should have come from the Essenes, if, as Harvey Falk, a New York rabbi, affirms, it was their role to introduce the commandments of Noah to the Gentiles. These com-mandments are contained in the second-century BC Book of Noah and form a less demanding code than that of Leviticus. In both cases it is satisfying to think that, with the law, came the angels who aid and supervise the keeping of its strictures. In essence they amount to the Golden Rule, formulated by Christ and by his contem-porary, the Pharisiacal teacher Ben Hillel, who declared 'what is hateful to yourself do not do to your neighbour. That is the entire Torah. All the rest is commentary.'

Each man's guardian angel helps him to understand

that law in every situation and protects him from those evil forces that would divert him from the commandment. Beyond these personal angels is the magnificent company of the seven archangels led by Michael and including the familiar names of Uriel, Rafael and Gabriel. Somewhere in the hierarchy between the two ranks of spirits are the intermediary messengers, seen and heard by men at important turning points in their lives.

The angels could appear in the form of human beings. So the obligation to extend hospitality to strangers was strengthened by the belief that one might be entertaining an angel unawares. Sometime a sign might be given, as it was to Cuthbert while he was serving as a guest master in Ripon. A beautiful but travel-worn wayfarer asked hospitality of the monastery. Cuthbert first offered him washing water and then left his guest to see to the preparation of a meal for him. When he returned the man had vanished and the only sign that anyone had been in the guest chamber were three loaves of the finest flour.

We do not know, from that story, what message the angel brought Cuthbert, unless it was a general confirmation of his faith and an assurance that the watchers were guiding and protecting him. His earlier experience of an angelic vision had been more specific and dramatic. It led directly to his firm decision to abandon the secular life and to follow a monastic vocation by asking to be admitted to Melrose Abbey. Cuthbert was a very young man at the time when, on the day of the death of Aidan, the first abbot of Lindisfarne, he saw in the sky above the Lammermuir Hills glorious, unearthly lights which consolidated into angelic forms.

Cuthbert's understanding of angels can only have come to him across the centuries from the elements of the Jewish tradition as they were emphasized by the Celtic Church. The liturgy he learnt and the scriptures he revered came from the same source; and they had been the mainstay of the Irish Church for some 300 years before he entered the abbey of Old Melrose in the woods above the Tweed. The psalms which he chanted regularly and at great length, and which Jerome (who translated them into Latin) claimed that people sang as they went about their work in homes and gardens, came from the Hebrew Psalter. The Jewish musical tradition can even give us some idea of the sounds they made.

In the third century a hundred years before Jerome produced the Vulgate version of the Scriptures, Jewish scholars in Alexandria translated at least half the Bible into Greek. The rest followed in the course of the next 200 hundred years. Although the story goes that seventy-two learned Jews all worked independently to produce identical versions of the Septuagint, which drew its name from their labours, it is hard to imagine that this devoted act of scholarship was not completed without a great deal of debate and discussion. Whether this is so or not, the production of the Greek Bible took place at a time when the rabbinical schools were forging the Talmud and the Midrash, commentaries on the sacred words of the Torah, the law of God. The first Jewish Christians, the Minims, who still attended synagogue and who were even asked to preach there, must have been affected by all this scholarly activity.

Alexandria was the hub of the religious debate that ensued. It was in this great cosmopolitan and cultured city that the most learned Jews settled after the destruction of the Temple. Greek, the language in which synagogue services were held outside the Holy Land, was the *lingua franca*. And it was here that the Christian fathers were attempting to build a universal church and to formulate an enduring creed, in the recognition that they had been mistaken in expecting a rapid end to the world and an immediate second coming of Christ.

In doing so they built on the tradition of the Jews, with whom they were in constant dialogue. The Christian *agape* or love feast (not to be confused with the Eucharist) had many parallels with the ritual of Jewish supper, the Chabûrah, held on Friday and Saturday evenings and at certain festivals. In both rituals the leader of the feast performed the initial grace by taking the bread, then blessing and eating a small piece, before giving fragments to everyone at the table. Each participant at the feast blessed his own wine.

The food that was eaten at both Jewish and Christian feasts must have been similar in the early centuries when the Minims naturally observed the Jewish dietary laws; but as the *agape* came to be celebrated by the Gentiles, and especially by the Celtic Britons, divergencies would have crept in. Celts had no compulsion against eating the meat of pigs. Indeed, the boar was a Celtic totem animal, and as such its flesh was ritually consumed at the great druidic feasts; legends of heroic boar hunts usually end in orgies of roast pork. Perhaps it was this consideration that was to turn so many Celtic monks into vegetarians. I shall have more to say about this in chapter 5.

Meanwhile I should like to reflect on the music that was an essential part of both Jewish and Christian festivities. In the Jewish tradition, singing and dancing went together, as we find them in the description of the song of Miriam in Exodus, and in the apocryphal Acts of St John, which tells of Christ and his disciples taking part in a round dance (or carol, as such singing and dancing activity came to be called in English Middle Ages) at the conclusion of the Last Supper.

What tunes and harmonies were sung? Although the central feature of Temple music was the singing of the Psalms, no written version survives. However, the construction and balance of the verses and placing of the repetitions give us an idea of the rhythmic structure of the music; and Philo's declaration that Moses was instructed in the sciences and in music by Egyptian priests suggests that Jewish music would have taken Coptic form and be akin to what we know of North

African sounds. Certainly the Levites, who came to be regarded as a caste of sacred musicians, feared the effects of what they considered to be degenerate Greek music and discouraged the congregations from having any contact with it. This meant that the former use of the drum, the lute and the harp in synagogue services was discontinued. Only the ram's horn was retained.

In the puritanical setting of those services the Jewish cantillation of prayers and of the Scriptures was emphasized. It was to become the basis of early Christian plainsong, and although the earliest manuscript of it that we possess dates from the third century we can be sure that music formed part of the Christian liturgy before that. In the same way as Jewish music influenced Christian hymns, so did the pattern of Sabbath worship in the synagogue affect the structure of the Christian Sunday morning liturgy. In both traditions the morning services included a sermon which followed the Jewish Midrash in providing an explanation of the Scriptures or an exhortation based on them.

Yet again the Golden Rule had primacy. It was more fundamental than the liturgy and formed an identical philosophy of daily living that both Jews and Christians could share. For those Jews who believed that God had allowed the destruction of the Temple in order to punish his people for their waywardness, there was the consolation that reparation could be made through *hesed*, acts of loving kindness and mercy, which would restore a right balance to personal relationships.

Thus the two religions grew together, and some notions of the ideas being discussed on the shores of the Mediterranean must have reached these islands and been known to the small Jewish communities who lived in Britain at the time of the Romans. There is a strong possibility that there was a synagogue in the Roman garrison town of Colchester; and Gildas tells us that a man named Aaron was among the Christian martyrs at

Caerleon, which suggests that there too the Minims made up part of the congregation. Those Christian Jews would have influenced the surrounding Celts even if members of the Colchester congregation at least were more confined to the society of the legions.

Yet, quite apart from any theological ideas that may have been formulated, the Jewish and Celtic races had several natural affinities, mostly to do with rhythms of time. It was an affinity that was to take on massive proportions in the seventh century, when Rome determined to control the British Church. Both Celts and Jews counted time by nights rather than by days, by dark rather than by light, as in 'The evening and the morning were the first day'; and on the analogy of that, they both started the year with the onset of winter. Furthermore, they both used a lunar calendar, giving a twelve-month year of four weeks to a month with an extra four-week month every nineteenth year to mop up the discrepancies.

Although I have found no reference to any Jews living in this country after the departure of the Romans, there is every reason to believe that any remaining community would have been acceptable to the emerging Celtic Church. It was not until the Emperor Julian made an alliance with the Jews, when he turned against Christianity, that there was any hostility between the two faiths. One prejudice entered the dialogue it persisted and increased. John Chrysostom, Patriarch of Constantinople, took a strong anti-Semitic stand in his discourses; and he was the beloved teacher of John Cassian, whose monastic foundation in Gaul was to influence similar settlements in Ireland and mainland Britain.

In 414 the Christians in Alexandria actually rioted against the Jews, and from that time on hostility persisted. Right through the Middle Ages Jews were used and scorned. Yet Chrysostom had felt it necessary to dissuade the Christians at Antioch from observing Jewish customs and ceremonies. Now, with the appalling shadow of the Holocaust presenting Jew and Gentile alike with a tragedy beyond the grasp of most men's minds, Jews and Christians are coming together again. Freed at last from the compulsion to evangelize, the Christian Churches are entering into a renewed dialogue with the Jews, and even readopting some of their rituals and festivals. One Dorset church has even initiated the practise of holding the Jewish Feast of the Tabernacles instead of the traditional harvest thanksgiving. The object of both ceremonies is the same.

The agricultural relevance of the Feast of Tabernacles is implied in its other Jewish name, the Feast of Ingathering; but it is as 'Tabernacles' that the festival is especially relevant to the Celtic Church. Modern Jews observe this feast in obedience to Leviticus (23, 42–3): 'Ye shall dwell in booths seven days; all that are Israelites born shall dwell in booths: that your generations may know that I made the children of Israel to dwell in booths, when I brought them out of the land of Egypt; I am the Lord your God.'

There is some discussion as to whether 'booths' refers to the cloud that protected the children of Israel by day and gave them light at night as they wandered in the wilderness, or whether the word is to be taken in a literal sense. The booths are the rough huts of a travelling people, now symbolized by the *succah*, which each practising Jew enters during the eight days of the festival. This is now a decorated bower, but it stands for a makeshift dwelling, a reminder that, however secure we may feel ourselves to be, we have no abiding place on earth in our seemingly solid houses of bricks and mortar.

As we shall see, this concept was particularly close to the hearts of Celtic Christians who married an instinctive love of wandering to the religious feeling that trust in God's protection was best evinced by a sense of impermanence. They probably knew little of the Jewish feasts, but they certainly knew the Bible, and they likened their own journeys to Abraham's response to God's command to 'get thee out of thy country, and from thy kindred, and from thy father's house,' (Genesis, 12, 1).

The Celts also identified with the wanderings of the chosen people as Moses led them out of Egypt. But it is to Egypt that we must return, for it was there, as we have seen, that during the first four centuries Judaism and Christianity took the form by which we know them today.

I hope I am not being too cynical in suggesting that in those early centuries in Egypt Jews and Christians were also linked by the strongest of bonds: a common enemy. At the beginning of the third century Origen, who, according to Jerome, 'knew the scriptures by heart and toiled night and day at studying their explanation', wrote his most famous work, a confrontation of the Roman cynic Celsus, who attacked Jews and Christians alike. The urbane Celsus contented himself with words; but as the might of the Roman Empire approached disintegration, the followers of any religion who refused to acknowledge the divinity of Caesar went in danger of physical violence, slavery and death.

The Copts

Before the canon of the New Testament was formed in the fourth century, and before the Church had defined its doctrine in creeds, the early Christian fathers remained in dialogue with the rabbis. Clement of Alexandria, Origen's teacher, held firmly to many tenets of the Jewish tradition. He declared his belief in the angelic host with the statement: 'To nations and cities have been assigned the regiment of angels; and perhaps even some of them of one type may have been set aside for individuals.' Yet Clement was also greatly influenced by Greek philosophy, and in his writings one feels that the word 'angels' could often be replaced by the Platonic 'aeons' or 'emanations'.

Both Clement and Origen (whose works were later declared anathema) can be described as Gnostics, for they gained a posthumous involvement in the first of the many heresies which ironically enabled the Church to define its dogma. For it was in refuting the heresies that successive councils of bishops forged the creed which came to establish the differing authorities of Rome and Constantinople in the fourth and fifth centuries.

Between these two papal cities lay the oldest Christian authority, the Church of Ethiopia and Egypt, which came to conduct its services in the ancient language of the pharoahs, called Coptic by the Arabs. This Church's claim to have been founded by Mark was as strong as that made by Rome for its foundation by Peter. According to legend, the evangelist converted the first Egyptian, a cobbler, whose name is given as Annainos, by healing his wounded hand.

Whether or not the Coptic Church grew out of that miracle, it is certain that the gospel of Mark, differing from the canonical Gospel of that evangelist, was known in Egypt. Clement claimed that it was written in Alexandria after the death of Peter; and he tells us that on Mark's death, this 'secret gospel' was carefully guarded by the Egyptian Christians and could be read only by those who were being initiated into the great mysteries. Clement claimed that these words of Mark formed 'a more spiritual gospel' for the use of those who were being perfected, and that it included sayings which led into 'the innermost sanctuary of the truth'.

That claim for a special scripture for the initiates leads us immediately into the realm of Gnosticism. This doctrine of salvation by knowledge, as it was understood by those Christian fathers who opposed it, implied a strict hierarchy, but it was one that could also be considered as a ladder. This hierarchy was based on the different levels by which the scriptures could be interpreted; and these scriptures included the Old Testament and such apocryphal writings as the Book of Enoch, together with the many scrolls out of which the canon of the New Testament was eventually formed at the beginning of the fourth century.

For the simple-minded reader of those scriptures, or the fundamentalist as we might today describe him, the words of Holy Writ had to be revered for their literal meaning; the pious and the scholarly could regard them as in some sense metaphorical and allegorical, looking to the ethical teaching behind the literal story; but only the truly spiritual could grasp the vital inner meaning of the words. Both Clement and Origen believed that with the

The Lion, symbol of St. Mark. Gospel of St. Matthew. Book of Kells.

grace of God, each sincere Christian should strive to attain the ultimate state of Gnosticism; and Origen in particular showed by the dedicated rigour and ardour of his own life that such a quest for spiritual understanding did not excuse the Christian from obedience to the literal interpretation of the law and from adherence to the moral code.

The Gnosticism which flourished in Egypt was seen as a threat to the established Church because it brought with it the uncontrollable element of individual insight into the divine purpose. In the same way the Church in Rome was to feel threatened by the heresy introduced in the fourth century by the British monk Pelagius, who denied the inevitability of original sin, and who emphasized the importance of individual willpower combined with grace. The authority of the Church demanded that salvation should be through grace alone and reserved to itself the right to determine how that grace should be revealed. It was a position that the early Gnostics and later the Pelagians were bound to undermine.

Before the latter heresy erupted, even more serious divisions relating to the most fundamental tenets of the Church were causing bitter disputes, leading even to physical violence among the Christians of Egypt and North Africa. The quarrels arose out of that fundamental question which every person in every generation of a Christian inheritance still has to struggle with: 'But what think ye of Christ?' Is he man or God, and if both, how do these natures combine?

It is a question whose answer lies beyond the reach of human logic, and there will always be those who attempt to resolve it by stressing either the humanity of the historical person of Jesus or the divinity of the cosmic Christ beyond space and time. The heresy propounded by Arius of Libya stressed the humanity of Jesus to the extent of declaring that the Son could not be co-equal with the Father, and so denying the validity of the Christian Trinity. His philosophy spread widely, for he put his ideas into metrical hymns that could be sung by the simple and enthusiastic. Perhaps there is an echo of his teaching in the 'gentle Jesus' hymns of our forefathers and in some of the more catchy numbers of the evangelical movements today.

Arius was declared a heretic at the first Council of Nicaea in 325, but his ideas persisted up to the sixth century and drew adherents as far afield as Spain. The Arian propositions were countered by the Monophysites, who stressed the divine nature of Christ at the expense of the humanity of Jesus. This view of the godhead was to have a powerful influence on the Coptic Church, and from that source it moulded much of the thinking of the fifth-century Church in Ireland.

The argument for Monophysitism, which concentrated on the spirit, led to a mysticism that had much in common with the doctrines of the Gnostics. The Church reacted against this latter heresy for many of the same reasons as it had renounced the former. It was Monophysitism that presented the greater threat, however, for its emphasis on the awe and mystery surrounding the figure of Christ questioned the historical event of the incarnation that had brought the Church into being.

The matter was resolved to the satisfaction of the orthodox at the Council of Chalcedon in 451. The victory of the authoritarian Church in the Middle East was no more universally welcome then than the outcome the Synod of Whitby was to be in Britain 200 years later. There were many dissenters after Chalcedon and some devoted adherents of Monophysitism fled out of Egypt rather than deny their doctrine. Others remained, but, in defiance of the council's ruling, incorporated their beliefs into the Coptic Church, so cutting it off from the rest of Christendom in much the same way as some pockets of the Irish Church went their own way after the Synod of Whitby gave supreme power to Rome. After Chalcedon the Patriarch of Constantinople always had precedence over the Patriarch of Alexandria; and the Church in Egypt gradually loosened its linguistic and liturgical ties with Greece and became exclusively Coptic in the conduct of its affairs.

It must have been about this time that the seven Coptic monks whose bodies were buried in Ireland, according to a tenth-century document, spread their doctrines throughout that country. They could hardly have been the first Egyptians to go there, and there can be little doubt that Irish monks also made their way to Egypt. They must have been doing so for centuries. How else could Origen have learned of the Christian communities in those parts of Britain into which Rome never penetrated? Yet any Irish monks who visited Egypt in the fifth century would surely have been less concerned with the subtleties of doctrine than with the extraordinary austerity with which their counterparts were conducting their lives.

Pilgrims from all over the known world were coming to Egypt at that time to witness the dedication of the desert Christians, and to obtain a few wise words from them that would help them in the conduct of their own lives and direct them in their search for truth. The wisdom they were seeking came from men who voluntarily cut themselves off from human companionship and the constant encouragement of their fellow Christians by going out into the wastelands of the desert. In so doing they were to provide a symbol that has been used many mystics down the ages. Time and again the geographical location of the desert has been used as an image of the arid emptiness of the spiritual place in which the soul finds itself when faith is withdrawn. For Celtic pilgrims, these old men of the desert of Egypt must have been recognized as soul friends or spiritual guides in a way that could have been understood by the druid priests.

The self-imposed austerities of the desert fathers began when the Roman persecutions stopped. After Constantine's Edict of Milan in 313 it was a simple matter to profess Christianity openly. In fact, the state probably offered a more comfortable life to those who professed this now respectable religion than to those who clung on to Pagan beliefs. This did not suit the ardent Egyptians, who had hammered out their faith in the schools of Alexandria and wished to prove their emotional as well as their intellectual commitment to their beliefs.

So it came about that groups of believers went off into the desert to live lives of physical frugality and constant prayer. These early hermits usually lived in separate cells, grouped round a common water supply. On Sundays, the one day on which they met to worship together, they each took back sufficient water to last the week. The first such cluster of cells was founded at Scete, a swamp in the Nile Delta. The community that came into being there provided a long-lasting model for the semi-eremetic life. It still pertains today.

Then, as now, some people still sought even greater isolation. They left the group to seek out solitary hermitages at a great distance from their fellow men, following the example of Antony, who lived twenty years alone on the deserted hill fort of Pispir. The attraction of this way of life began to be so compulsive that a writer of that time declared that the desert was becoming more populous than the cities. An exaggeration, of course, but his petulance provokes the thought that some hermits at least must have sought the desert in the same spirit which drives many people today to leave the turbulence of the inner cities. It is almost blasphemy to suggest that in some instances men may have chosen desert cells and caves rather than face the plagues and pestilences that were rife in the crowded parts of Alexandria and the other cities round the Nile delta, yet it may well have been so.

That admitted, it would be a mistake to over-emphasize this negative aspect of the impulse to a solitary life. The majority of the desert hermits were not primarily motivated by a desire to save their own skins. It was not that sort of prudence which drew hundreds of pilgrims to seek them out and to undertake long and hazardous journeys in order to do so. The hermits of the Egyptian desert were anxious to save their souls rather than their bodies and would go to inordinate lengths to resist the powers of evil that manifested themselves through the flesh. Although they were equally concerned for the whole of humanity they did not evangelize. The faithful had to come to them, and even then they were chary of their words, obeying the laws of hospitality and giving physical sustenance to all comers, but only talking at any length to genuine seekers for truth.

Because they were so selective, their words were treasured. The *apophthegmata* (sayings to live by) were collected and preserved in Coptic, Syriac and Greek as *The Sayings of the Desert Fathers*. Throughout the early Middle Ages these sayings, grouped according to subject, were widely translated and disseminated. The best of them read now like the wise and pithy tales and parables told by the Jewish Hasidim of the eighteenth century in Eastern Europe; but too many are filled with a desperate fear of the wrath to come and a propitiatory compulsion to try to avoid it by living lives of continual misery. 'We have to give an account of our whole life in the presence of heaven and earth, and you are able to laugh,' declared one old man when he saw someone merry. Another said, 'Just as we carry our own shadow everywhere with us, so we ought also to have tears and compunction with us wherever we are.'

Living so, and determined to cut themselves off from the pleasures of the flesh, they were naturally tormented by greed and lust. Many of their stories tell how the devil used these weapons to tempt them. Sometimes they fell. When that happened they had little charity for themselves, but they had comforting words for their erring brothers, only ignoring the injunction to 'judge not' when it applied to themselves. So they did not condemn their fellows but patiently exhorted them to continue their struggle against the demons who had sent the fatal temptations. In practical terms their kindness went to such lengths that Abba Macarius, the founder of Scete, actually took a 60-mile journey to Alexandria in order to get honeycakes for a sick monk.

Throughout all the sayings of the desert fathers there is, as one would expect, an emphasis on silence and stillness. They sought these states in order to become a Hesychast and enter into perpetual prayer.

Like the Jesus prayer of the Orthodox Church, the Catholic *Ave Maria*, and even Mother Thérèsa's prayer which had been adopted by the Peace Movement, the simple, oft-repeated words they used were a way of centring the heart on God and transcending temporal cares. To still thoughts of worldly affairs they might recite the whole Psalter; and this was an exercise adopted by the Celtic saints, whose biographers recount their ascetic practice of mortifying the flesh by standing for long hours in cold water as they sang out the holy verses.

Like the Jews, the hermits of the Egyptian desert stood to pray, elbows close to their sides and their palms uplifted. This is the stance still adopted by members of the Coptic Church, and it is how we can imagine men like Cuthbert praying as the cold waves of the sea broke round their legs.

Yet even a solitary man cannot give his whole time to the outward forms of prayer. He has to cultivate a little land to provide himself with some sustenance or produce goods that can be exchanged for food. Many of the desert hermits spent their working time twisting ropes and weaving rush mats and baskets. Even inessential work was advocated, for physical labour could still distracting thought and wayward desires. So we read stories of totally useless drudgery being undertaken solely for the purpose of dulling the mind to the concerns of the world.

The practice, which they also adopted, of dedicating essential daily activities, however minute, to God is more attractive. It was a way of bringing a full conscious awareness and responsibility into every aspect of life. The Essene manual of discipline, which would have been known to the desert hermits through the Egyptian Therapeutae, advocated constant worship: 'At the beginning of each of my daily tasks, when I leave or enter the house, when I rise, when I stretch out on my couch, Him do I wish to celebrate.'

Such constant worship was general throughout the early Church as it was among faithful Jews – as we can see in the Hebrew Prayer Book's benedictions for all sorts of occasions from smelling fragrant oils, drinking wine, looking at the sea or a beautiful animal or tree, to seeing wise men and hearing good tidings. It proved to be natural to the Celtic mind as well, which, with the coming of Christianity, formed special prayers to be used almost in the form of protective charms for every activity from *smooring* (the covering of the peat fire) in the evening to putting one's clothes on in the morning.

There is the danger that such habitual graces can become mechanical or imbued with superstition as the supplicant comes to dread the disasters that will follow if he forgets the order of words. That was not the purpose of the desert fathers. Abba Agathon spoke for them all when he said, 'Prayer is hard work and a great struggle to one's last breath.' In looking at the way in which the Celtic Church used and adapted its inheritance, I shall be mindful of the life which its saints breathed into the dry bones of doctrine.

TWO

The Work

— 4 —

Scribes and Artists

All three sources that formed the Celtic Church come together in the artefacts that remain to us: the glories of Irish manuscript art, the intricacies of jewelry and metalwork, and the iconography of the engraved stones.

From the designs on the Neolithic megaliths and monuments such as that at New Grange comes the exuberant patterning of spirals, chevrons and the decorative fern-like motifs that adorn the manuscript pages of the Celtic gospels; and the druidic priests contributed the legacy of the stiff Ogham strokes used on some early grave stones. From the Jewish inheritance comes the obvious dedication of the scribes who undertook the work of transcription, for, like the biblical scribes whose life and work were set apart for God, the monks in the scriptoria of the Celtic Church worked with a patient devotion. Finally the Coptic Church contributed the Eastern and Byzantine influence apparent in so much Celtic design.

The inscribed roll of the Torah is a living thing. Like a person, it is nine months in the making, and when the parchment becomes old and worn with use, it is not simply thrown away but given a proper and reverential burial. Fortunately for us, the monks of the Celtic Church showed the same reverence for their carefully and beautifully transcribed gospel books, so that, although many have been destroyed through the centuries, enough remain to delight and inspire us, as well as to show us something of what we have lost.

The flourish of manuscript art in north Britain and Ireland between the sixth and eighth centuries is a remarkable phenomenon. Nothing comparable was taking place elsewhere in Europe, and yet the need to copy and distribute the Gospels and mass books was surely as vital in Christian Gaul as it was in the monastic colleges of Ireland. The end of all this artistic activity is as puzzling as its beginning, for by the ninth century, when the authority of the Roman bishops had clamped down on the native Church, the traditions of monastic and ecclesiastic art were diverted into other channels. None of them, with the possible exception of stained glass, was to produce so rich a harvest.

The unbroken, even flow of the script is the first thing to strike anybody looking at an opening of a Celtic codex, whether this be the very early Book of Durrow and the well-known Book of Kells in the library of Trinity College, Dublin, the Lindisfarne Gospels in the British Museum; or the Book of Chad in Lichfield Cathedral. Most reproductions naturally concentrate on the illuminated pages, some of which are completely filled with abstract designs and symbols. Yet even the unadorned pages of the text show something equally remarkable: the steady lines of clear, cursive writing. The Irish script is a marvellous development from Roman lettering; and the manuscripts owe their existence to this flowing and orderly half-uncial style.

The work had to be done with painstaking care. Although the need for transcriptions was felt to be urgent, nothing was to be done in a hurry. Columba's first biographer, Adomnan, abbot of Iona, whose scriptorium probably produced the Book of Kells, implored 'all those who may wish to copy these books, nay more, I adjure them through Christ, the judge of all the ages, that, after carefully copying, they compare them with the examplar from which they have written, and emend them with the utmost care.' Like the Jewish scribes, who always had to copy one scroll from another, the Christian monks were forbidden to rely on memory.

Their patient calligraphy provided a sound basis for the vitality and inventiveness of the flourishes which decorated the capitals, adorned the margins and filled the heraldic initial pages. It is in that work that the influence of both pagan Celtic and Christian Coptic art is most apparent. The decorative modes of Irish manuscript art bring the Aryan and Semitic strands in the Celtic race together. On the one hand, the Indo-European heritage is manifest in the swirling spirals and the twisting, sinuous creatures which adorn the text; on the other, the influence of Byzantine and North African design can be seen in the so-called 'carpet' pages which interleaf the gospels.

An even more delicate legacy of Coptic art can be detected in the motif of ornamental red dots. These are always arranged in threes and sometimes used to accentuate the outline of letters. Produced from tiny drops of red lead, they must have taken hours to apply; yet over 10,000 of them are used for the initial page of St Luke in the Lindisfarne Gospels.

There is also a resemblance between the manuscript art of the Celtic Church and the garnet-encrusted metalwork of the Saxon jewellers discovered at Sutton Hoo and the interlaced, engraved patterning on the Anglican crosses at Bewcastle in Northumberland and at Rothwell on the Solway Firth. The Scandinavian invaders shared a common Indo-European ancestry with the British Celts, whose land they seized. In their art, it is apparent.

For Celtic manuscript art owed much to the long tradition of metalwork and jewelry that went before any

The portraits of the Evangelists from the Lindisfarne Gospels.
Marygate House, Holy Island.

scribe took up his quill. As early as the third century BC there was a flourishing school of silver smithing in Pictish Scotland. At the same time, the classical nations were learning enamelling from the Celts, who poured brilliant colours on heated brass. Much of the Celtic jewelry, such as the gold brooch from Tara, now in the museum of the Irish Academy, confirms the strong resemblance between the interweaving designs of the manuscript decorations and the devices of goldsmiths and jewellers who were plying their craft many centuries earlier.

This does not mean that the jewellers who were attached to Christian communities could not be as inventive as their forebears. From Irish *crannogs*, lake villages settled in the Christian era, ox bones have been discovered which carry engraved blueprints for subsequent metalwork. The skill that these craftsmen possessed is proved in the hoard of eighth-century silver unearthed on St Ninian's Isle, Shetland, when an early church was being excavated. The animals decorating one of the bowls in that collection are the same delicately convoluted creatures that adorn the manuscripts.

Records show that monks in the monasteries of Iona and Lindisfarne who were crafted as metalworkers were also engaged in adorning the manuscripts in the scriptoria. The earliest example of tooled bookbinding to come down to us is the decorated red leather cover of a tiny Gospel of St John. It was discovered in Cuthbert's coffin at the time of the rebuilding of Durham Cathedral in 1104. Sadly, the jewelled binding, worked by the anchorite Billfrith for the leather cover of the Lindisfarne Gospels, has been lost to us, but we know of its existence from the colophon that the priest Aldred added to the manuscript when it came to Chester-le-Street, when the monks fleeing with Cuthbert's body and the treasures of Lindisfarne came to rest there.

However, it was not the bindings, but the boxes in which the precious books were stored which gave the jewellers most scope for the exercise of their craft. For as the Jews keep the Torah meticulously housed, so the Celts guarded the holy words of gospel and missal. They used elaborate jewel-encrusted boxes, and examples of these are displayed in the museums of Dublin and Edinburgh.

The same art that adorned the manuscript cases is also evident in the remaining reliquaries in which the relics of the saints were carried. In those little altar-shaped boxes the bones of the holy men were honoured. They formed a focus of intercession, and it was believed that through them the saint in Heaven could help believers on earth. So in the bitter wars between the Scots and the English fragments of the bones of Columba were carried into the battle of Bannockburn, housed in a brilliant blue jewelled box, now in the Museum of Antiquities in Edinburgh, but which stood for many centuries in the church of Monymusk in Aberdeenshire.

Like the reliquaries, the manuscripts could also be regarded as talismen possessed of miraculous healing powers. In 1627 Connel MacGeoghegan, who translated the annals of Clonmacnoise, a monastery site on the banks of the Shannon not far from Durrow, told of the 300 books which Columba is said to have written with his own hand. The translator claimed that the saint left a copy of each of these books to every church with which he had been associated in Ireland,

> which Bookes have a strange property, which is that if they or any of them had sunck to the bottom of the deepest waters they would not loose one letter, signe of character of them, which I have seen partly myselfe of that book of them which is at Dorrow ... for I saw the ignorant man that had the same in his custody, when sickness came upon cattle, for their remedy putt water on the book and suffered it to rest there a while and saw alsoe cattle returne thereby to their former or pristin state and the book receave no loss:

Stories about the manuscripts' resistance to water is common. Ninian's biographer claimed that the saint's custom was to read as he walked on his long journeys. As long as he concentrated on the text, the page would remain miraculously dry in the heaviest showers, but if he let his mind wander the book would be soaked. There is even a tradition that the Lindisfarne Gospels fell into the Solway Firth when the monks fleeing westwards from the Danes planned to take the holy book to Ireland. Storms prevented them from making the crossing and the manuscript fell into the waves only to be miraculously washed ashore unharmed.

The dome-shaped bronze handbells used by the wandering saints to assemble the people together in hillside or river bank were treated with similar reverence and frequently enclosed in elaborate metal shrines. Some of these were made long after the original owners had died, and were adorned with symbols, such as the crucifix, which were not used by the Celtic Church. Its sign was the ancient form of the cross embodied in the Wheel of Life, and as such it had no connection with a gallows.

It was after the Synod of Whitby, when the Irish Church had come under the authority of Rome, that the tall stone crosses were erected outside the monastic churches. Yet even they have pagan links as well as retaining much of the influence of the Celtic Church. The stone Anglian crosses of the Scottish Borders grew out of Yggdrasil, the Scandinavian Tree of Life, an impression that is not denied by the Christian words of *The Dream of the Rood*, a poem partly inscribed in runic characters in the cross that is now kept in the church at Rothwell. That poem celebrates Christ as a Saxon hero, hanging on the tree, as the myths tell us Odin did, for the salvation of mankind. The courage of the young warrior was something that Celts and Saxons could celebrate together.

The Cross
of St. Piran

From: The Church of St. Piran, Perranzabuloe (Guide Book)
(drawn by Alice C. Butler, reproduced by permission of the Vicar
of Perranzabuloe).

In using long-held pagan beliefs and attitudes to further the worship of Christ, the Church was only going one step farther from the practise of Christianizing pagan sites and building churches in places made sacred thousands of years before. The practice of adopting a prehistoric ritual standing stone for Christ was common. Right through Brittany you can find the tall menhirs of megalithic peoples inscribed with the cross.

The Celtic Church, like its Eastern counterpart, also used the T-shaped tau cross. On early manuscripts and later stone crosses a tau-headed crozier is often given to evangelist or abbot. It is both a pagan and a Jewish sign. At the National Museum in Dublin there is an Irish pre-Christian tau which brings two heads together, one on each arm of the cross. It may mark a truce brought about between two warring tribes. It certainly reminds us of the Celtic reverence for the severed head as a seat of power. The Jewish symbol of the tau, linked to the sacred name of God, made the sign acceptable to the Church. When tau crosses appear in manuscript it is usually in conjunction with a more familiar crozier. So in the Lichfield Gospels or Book of Chad St Luke appears with a tau in his right hand, a cross in his left.

In sculpture one of the finest examples of a tau cross is seen in the centre of the so-called Cross of the Scriptures at Clonmacnoise. The wheel cross which surmounts this tall stone has, for its central figure, the form of a man, who may be taken to be Christ. Like St Luke in the manuscript, he holds a tau-headed rod in his right hand, a crozier in his left. Below the cross are three panels depicting scenes from the Bible, and the pedestal is a frieze of horses and charioteers.

The carvings of the high cross at Clonmacnoise are deliberately biblical, but the remarkable feature of many such tall crosses is the combination of secular carvings with the Christian motifs and icons. Unlike the weird and wonderful gargoyles of the medieval cathedrals and the strange beasts and decorative plants of the manuscript illustrations, the figures' engraved on the stones are realistic. They can be seen at their best on the seventh-and eighth-century Pictish stones of northeast Scotland. Some of these have been gathered into museums; others stand by the roadside.

On one side of these stones the religious motifs are displayed in a stark iconography. The wheel cross is frequently flanked by stylized angels, and the figures of Antony and Paul being fed by ravens in the Egyptian desert is a favourite theme. The other side is often quite different. In minute detail, which enables us to reconstruct the dress and manners of the times, we find hunting scenes and battles depicted on the stones.

For some time after the decision of Whitby, the Pictish communities remained loyal to the Irish Church of Iona to which they owed their conversion. It is from this period that the stones originate. Their comparatively late date makes the other feature they possess all the more puzzling, for among the traces of late Ogham script and the Christian symbols are some often repeated mysterious figures. The Z-shaped rods, the long-snouted swimming beasts which would look like elephants if their trunks did not sprout from between their ears, and the designs that resemble a mirror and comb were all peculiar to this lost people, but they must have been familiar throughout the Church in Scotland at least.

The earliest stones to carry a purely Christian message are naturally the grave stones of the faithful. On some of these a fine-cut Latin inscription giving the names of the dead is combined with short incisions using the vertical strokes of the Ogham script. There are examples of this in Cornwall and Wales as well as in Ireland and Scotland. An impressive collection of pre-Whitby stones, commemorating church leaders of a very early date, stands in the porch of the ruined church of Kirkmadrine on the Rhinns of Galloway.

In Clonmacnoise another series of early stones are movingly displayed. They have none of the pomp of the Romano-British memorials in Scotland, for they carry only a roughly carved wheel cross. Sometimes the names of the dead are given, and on one or two of the stones this is combined with an inscription asking that the translated spirit will pray for his fellows on earth. Sometimes this inscription is accompanied by an *orans*, an image of the departed soul at prayer.

Yet on the whole the Celtic Church was more concerned with celebrating life than recording death. Every living thing, from the domestic cat and kittens which play among the Chi-Rho monogram at the beginning of St Matthew's Gospel in the Book of Kells, to the low-slung, dragon-like lion which heralds the words of St Mark in the Book of Chad and his more elegant counterpart in the Book of Armagh, testifies to the lively delight which the monks obviously took in the world around them. The exuberance of the illustrated pages, the jewelled caskets and the engraved stones does not speak of a puritanical rejection of life but of praise for nature's infinite variety.

— 5 —

Peace with Nature

The obvious delight that the scribes and craftsmen of the Celtic Church took in the world around them is reflected in the stories passed down through hagiographies and legends about the miraculous interaction between the saints and the animal kingdom. Although we do not have to believe that a horse produced food for Cuthbert from beneath a roof thatch, or that sea otters dried him after he had spent a night in the sea chanting psalms, we can be sure that such stories were told because he lived in harmony with the beasts. Such an attitude helped the people to lose their fear of a cruel and hostile nature which could only be placated by subservience to local gods, and freed them to regard our fellow creatures with a benevolent respect.

In none of the stories do we find that the saints adopted an arrogant 'Lords of Creation' stance towards the animals, even when they felt the need to rebuke them. Their affinity was much closer than that between an authoritarian master and a subservient slave or a piece of semi-animate clockwork. It stemmed from the shamanistic properties possessed by some of the druids, who had the ability to communicate and even identify with beasts.

A look at more recent folk history illustrates the kind of identifications with nature which enabled the saints of the Celtic Church to perform apparent feats of magic.

The well-known folklorist, George Ewart Evans, tells of the power of the horseman's word in northeast Scotland, the land of the Picts. As late as the nineteenth century a farmer or carter who was initiated into the Society of the Horseman's Word was given a secret 'mantra' as a symbol of his identity with the horse. This word was believed to have a psychic power, giving the man complete control over the horse, whom he nevertheless regarded as a fellow member of the society.

Such an identity between man and beast is reflected in the sorrow shown by the horse on Iona on the day that Columba died. When Adomnan recounted that story, he put the following words into Columba's mouth in response to those who wanted to drive the animal away: 'To this brute beast, devoid of reason, the Creator himself has in some way manifestly made it known that its master is about to leave it'.

The lives of the saints are full of such gentle tales of the affinity between men and beasts in an acknowledgement that every living creature owes its existence to God. When Columba's friend Kenneth complained that the noise of the seagulls distracted him from his devotions, the birds agreed to keep quiet all Sunday until matins on Monday morning. Beuno of Wales was tempted to put a similar structure on the croaking of the frogs, until he realized that their harsh voices could be as pleasing to the Almighty as his own lengthy chanting of the 119th Psalm.

Brendan's monks took a contrary view. They feared that the noise of their psalm-singing would disturb the birds, so they asked the saint if he would please sing with less gusto. Brendan stoutly refused. He sang louder than ever and was pleased to point out that the birds were joining in, in praise of their Creator. So saints and birds lived happily together, and a story, worthy of Edward Lear, is told about Kevin. As that great Irishman stood to pray, his arms outstretched in the Coptic manner, he found that a blackbird had made a nest in his hand.

Thereupon the saint went on standing still until the eggs had been laid and hatched and the fledglings were flown.

It was a curlew who helped Beuno to realize the protective power that looked after the sacred written word. We have already seen that water was unable to damage Holy Writ, so the saint should not have worried unduly when he dropped his sermon in the Menai Straits as he went over to preach on the druid-island of Anglesey from his college of Clynnog Fawr on the mainland. However, the matter was not to be put to the test. The seabird picked up the parchment and put it out of reach of the tide. In gratitude the saint prayed that the Creator would always take especial care of curlews, and that is why these birds make their nests in such hidden and inaccessible places.

There are other stories which tell of the trust that the saints put in the creatures to show them the will of God, and particularly to direct them to choose the right place for a monastic settlement. So Glasgow was reported to have been founded in its place because the young Kentigern placed the body of the aged Fergus in a cart drawn by unbroken oxen, determined to bury him wherever the animals should stop. The place proved to be an old cemetery on the banks of the Clyde which had once been blessed by Ninian. Here Kentigern, who had just set out from the monastic college of Culross on the Firth of Forth, hung his handbell on the branch of a tree and formed his own settlement.

As oxen decreed where Glasgow was to be founded, so a herd of wild swine are said to have determined the siting for the wattle church around which Glastonbury Abbey was built. And when Dubricius came to found his Herefordshire monastery, pigs led him along the River Wye to show him the place he should choose. A little to the south of that settlement at Archenfield, Tewdric, the saintly king of Tintern, was directed by stags to the place where he should live out his days as a hermit. In a similar way Ciaran of Clonmacnoise, the son of a Meath carpenter and wheelwright, was led by a stag to his hermitage on the shores of Lough Ree.

The psychological moral of stories such as these is that a person at a crossroads in his life does well to trust his instinctive animal nature to indicate the direction he should take. The pragmatic explanation is that, left to themselves, animals will eventually make for a water supply, without which no human settlement would be possible. Most probably the saints who followed where oxen, swine and stags led them were well aware of both the psychological and factual elements of their actions. They had a similar common-sense wisdom about the properties of plants, and their herbal remedies no doubt contributed to their just reputations as miracle healers. In that work they were following in the steps of the Therapeutae whose gifts were so well known to the Coptic Church. Again there is a double element. Because of their instinctive understanding of the properties of nature, the saints were able to relieve mental and physical sickness in ways that must have seemed truly miraculous to people suffering from the spasmodic outbreaks of the virulent yellow plague, as well as the natural ills and accidents of life. At the same time the hagiographers would have us believe that the saints were not averse to using their powers over the laws of nature, which extended to an ability to restore the dead to life, in order to score over their enemies. Columba is said to have proved his superiority to Brud's druid in that way, and a like tale is told of Samson.

When that Welsh saint journeyed through Cornwall on his way to Brittany he found men on Bodmin Moor, in the hundred of Trigg, who were worshipping an image. Immediately he made the mark of the cross on a nearby stone and then started to plead with the people, asking them to turn away from their pagan practices and come back to the one God. This the people roundly refused to do, but as they were arguing with the saint a young man of the tribe came by, driving a herd of wild horses. The crowd of disputing men caused the animals to panic, and in the confusion the lad was knocked off his own horse and lay lifeless on the ground. Then Samson was able to say to the tribesmen, 'Your image is not able to give aid to this dead man. But if you will promise me that you will utterly destroy this idol and no longer adore it, I, with God's assistance, will bring this dead man to life'. Then he prayed for two hours over the body, and at the end of that time the boy was seen to be alive and well.

That story is somewhat unfair, for in the panic induced by such accidents, as well as by the fear of epidemics and famine, people of all religions have always looked for protective talismen in objects thought to be infused with divine power. The Christian Celts were no exception. Holy men such as Fillan, who preached along the shores of Loch Tay, used specially charged holy stones to heal the sick. Sometimes these stones, such as those used by Columba in his contests with the Pictish druid, showed their extraordinary powers by being buoyant enough to float. Perhaps the Irishmen who ventured as far as Iceland in the eighth century had actually brought back the floating pumice stone to astound the people.

After their deaths the relics of the saints became talismen in their own right. Both the possessions and the bodies of the holy men were held to work miraculous cures for specific diseases. So the relics of Triduana, a fourth-century abbess and virgin, were supposed to be particularly effective in curing diseases of the eye because she had plucked out her own eyes rather than give in to the wiles of the prince who wanted to marry her.

Beyond such reported miracles and the superstitions of the frightened was the saints' undoubted ability as natural healers. The power lay in the assurance and authority of these men and woman, and in their wise observation of the laws of nature. This careful observation also gained them a reputation for prophecy such as the druids had engineered for themselves, and which was undoubtedly enjoyed by the Neolithic and Bronze Age priests who constructed their megalithic temples in such a way that the alignments followed the movements of the heavenly bodies and enabled them to predict eclipses. Columba used such an understanding of the winds and weather when he spoke to his followers about a crane who had lost her bearings when trying to contend with adverse conditions. 'Eventually she will land on the west bank of Iona,' he said with assurance, telling his monks that when she did so she was to be looked after for the space of three days, after which she would be strong enough to fly back to her home in Ireland. It was the quiet care for all the living things that infused the self-supporting settlements of the Celtic Church. We have much to learn from the way these people farmed the land and took care of their fellow creatures.

As Columba knew the state of the turbulent winds which would bring the exhausted crane to his island, so the much travelled Irish monks who crossed difficult waters in frail craft must have had that instinctive feel for wind and weather which is as essential to agriculture as it is to seamanship. From this they gained the knowledge that enabled them to foretell the weather, an ability which always seems miraculous to the less observant. But the saints were more than meteorological forecasters, for they interpreted states of weather as signs from God. Bad weather could be taken as an indication that there was something wrong with the way people were conducting their lives, whereas favourable conditions were a sign of God's grace.

They took the injunction in the eleventh chapter of Deuteronomy in all seriousness: those who love God will have plentiful crops and good pasture for their cattle. In practical terms love for God is shown by love for his creation and a proper care for the earth. The opposite of such love is not hate but greed. We see it to day in the vast destruction of the earth for immediate gain. I think particularly of the current, wholesale obliteration of the South American rain forests and of the money spent on destroying financially unprofitable food, while man-made famine wastes large areas of the globe.

The Celts were aware of the destructive nature of greed and would certainly have echoed Schumacher's dictum that 'the material needs of human beings are limited and in fact quite modest, even though our material *wants* know no bounds'. A right understanding of need is symbolized in a story told about Neot – the anonymous saint, his name simply means 'new' – who may have been King Alfred's half-brother. This holy man had a pool by his settlement in which three fish swam. Every day he ate one of the fish, and every morning there were still three fish swimming. One day the saint fell sick and did not feel like eating anything at all. Still three fish went on swimming in the pool. Eventually Neot's companions, hoping to tempt the saint to eat by offering a choice of dishes, cooked each fish in a different manner. When the saint saw what food was spread before him, he was aghast. Immediately he recovered sufficiently to order the three untouched dishes to be emptied into the water. At once the fish returned to life and swam away. Now restored to health, Neot went back to his practice of eating one of the inexhaustable supply each day.

That story also illustrates the common-sense attitude that the Celtic monks had to matters of diet and fasting. They were not strictly vegetarian, eating flock animals, fish and poultry from time to time. Their diet was never excessive, but neither were their austerities; and although they observed the Lenten fasts of their Church in addition to the regular days of abstinence on

Wednesdays and Fridays, these obligations were sub-servient to the laws of hospitality. When guests arrived good food was prepared and shared, the monks redressing the balance by cutting their own food down when they were alone again.

The story of Neot and the fish is an obvious parable. Other accounts of the attitude of the saints to their responsibility for the earth which nourished them are more direct. Even though it was an angel who urged Kevin to cultivate the wild slopes of the Wicklow hills, he declined the suggestion. 'I have no wish that the creatures of God should be moved because of me', he is reported as saying. 'My God can help that place in some other fashion. And, moreover, all the wild creatures on these mountains are my housemates, gentle and familiar with me, and they would be sad of this that thou has said.'

Kevin was adamant that a place be found where he could grow his crops without having to make devastating clearances. That was why his monastic settlement grew in Glendalough, the valley of the two lakes, whose rich meadows provided all the needs of his growing community.

Such care for nature was part of the affinity with animals demonstrated by the leaders of the Celtic Church. When Cuthbert was attempting to be self-supporting on Inner Farne, birds came and perched on his sprouting barley. Instead of throwing stones at them or contriving some device to scare them off, he spoke gently to them, saying, 'Why are you touching a crop you did not sow? Or is it maybe that you have more need of it than I? If you have God's leave, do what he allows you: but if not, be off, and do no more damage to what is not your own.' The biographer tells us that at those words the birds flew off and never trespassed on the corn again.

Perhaps the birds knew of Cuthbert's especial love of their kind, for by the time he set about cultivating Inner Farne he had already established the first bird sactuary there, refusing to let anybody harm the eider duck which inhabit those waters. These birds are still known as Cuddy's chickens, from the affectionate nickname given to the saint by the people of Northumbria.

The urbane Wilfrid, whose name nobody would presume to tamper with, was astonished when he visited Guthlac in his fenland hermitage and saw two birds perched on the saint's shoulders. The architect of the Synod of Whitby was gently rebuked for his surprise. 'Hast thou never learned, brother,' Guthlac said, 'in Holy Writ, that he who hath led his life after God's will, the wild beasts and wild birds will become more intimate with him.'

The intimacy with animals extended to plants and naturally affected the monks' methods of cultivation. They knew of no kill-all pesticides or inorganic fertilizers, but even in the sixth and seventh centuries people were beginning to adopt methods of agriculture which would provide a speedy return regardless of the harm that might be done on the way.

There is a story that once all the saints in Ireland came to Columba's Durrow to fast against God. They were furious with the Almighty because the penitents, whom they had put on bread and water to make reparation for their sins, all died. An angel came to rebuke the saints for their anger at what seemed to be a divine injustice. 'Wonder not if the bread and water cannot sustain the penitents today,' said the heavenly messenger. 'The fruits and plants of the earth have been devastated, so that there is neither strength nor force in them to support anyone. The falsehood and sin and injustice of men have robbed the earth with its fruits of their strength and force. When men were obedient to God's will the plants of the earth retained their proper strength. At that time water was no worse for sustaining anyone than milk is today.'

There is a clear indication here that, like the Jews of old, who believed that the land would prosper as long as

The Church of the Rock on a ledge above the upper lake.
From *Glendalough* by Kenneth MacGowan. (Drawing by Muriel
O'Connor, reproduced by permission of Kamac Publications,
Dublin).

they adhered to the laws of Jehovah, the Celts felt
strongly that adherence to the will of God could be
equated with obedience to the rhythms and harmonies
of the natural environments. If these were carelessly or
deliberately flouted, disaster was bound to result; whereas great good was sure to come of their observance.
Even if we do not share such a direct theological faith, it
is obvious that the way we are treating our living earth,
from the apparent indifference to the long-term effects
of nuclear waste to carelessness over industrial processes
of all sorts, is threatening us with catastrophe.

The monks of the Celtic Church must have often unwittingly followed the heresy of Pelagius, with its appeal to British pragmatism, as they forced their will to the unremitting tasks of the soil and to the care of the implements which they used in its cultivation, but they also realized that their work was directed and made possible by the grace of God, manifest through the course of nature. Our disrespect and lack of consideration for anything other than our will directed towards the means of immediate satisfaction has led us into a dangerous impasse. For the Pelagian 'I ought, therefore I will', we have substituted a technological maxim 'I can, therefore I must'. As the conservation movement warns people of the obvious disasters inherent in such careless disregard of ecological checks and balances it comes close to the feelings of the Celtic Church.

The people of that Church were able to feel a reliance on the saints to protect and guide them in their daily work, as they laboured, often in harsh and dangerous circumstances, to ensure the food supply. This reliance continued through the generations long after the original saints were dead. For centuries Brigid and Columba, two of the most celebrated saints of Ireland, were called on as protectors of the cattle, in which a man's wealth was counted. In the nineteenth century Alexander Carmichael, who collected and translated the Gaelic songs and poems from northwest Scotland and the Outer Hebrides, found many work songs connected with the herding and tending of dairy cows. The following verse is typical of many such, which ask the saints' blessing on the creatures and on the labours of the crofter:

> Come, Mary, and milk my cow,
> Come, Bride, and encompass her,
> Come, Columba the benign,
>   And twine thy arms around my cow.

From the Middle Ages to the time of Carmichael such songs invoking the help of the saints were being sung by people who were also half consciously propitating the old gods. These local deities were mingled in the ancestral memories of the people with those ancient folk who built the barrows and stone henges which were by then thought to be inhabited by the fairy *sidhe*. Farmers' wives, who would not hesitate to describe themselves as good Christians did not think twice about putting out saucers of milk for the little people, either as a thank offering for successful yields or as way of asking for help. If the milk, the fruit of the farm, should be drunk by a passing hedgehog or other wild creature, that surely did not lessen the validity of the offering. The nineteenth-century women who put the saucers outside their doors at night might be acting out of superstition, but they were also doing something which Brigid, Columba and all the saints of the Celtic Church would fully approve. They were acknowledging the interdependence of nature, and admitting that even their hardest work did not entitle them to exclusive rights to the fruits of the soil.

— 6 —

Brigid

Beyond Patrick, beyond Columba, beyond the kindly wisdom of Aidan and Cuthbert is Brigid, nun of Kildare. She is the Sophia/Mary spirit of the Celtic Church, giving form to the Jewish *Shekhina*, the feminine aspect of the presence of God. She is a triad in her own nature; Brigid, the earth goddess; Brigid, the nobly-fathered bastard girl who was to become a capable and powerful abbess; and Brigid, the mystical spirit, Mary's midwife and Christ's foster mother, who offers protection to mankind.

Brigid the goddess is herself threefold. She possesses the mercurial lightness of a girl, the benevolent practicality of the matron and the sharp, humorous wisdom of the crone. She is all women and all goddesses too. As well as being the gentle Brigid, she is also the powerful Brigantia to whom a whole territory in north Britain was dedicated. In Irish mythology she is usually described as the daughter of Dagda, the All Father; but Robert Graves considered she was the mother of all the gods. As the spirit of earth and nature, she can appear cruel as well as kind; in her support of life she employs both the destructive and life-enhancing qualities of fire and water.

The tending of a perpetual fire was part of the ritual of her worship. The flames that were once kept alight for

The ruined cathedral showing the round tower with conical
cap (right) and the remaining wall of Saint Brigid's fire house,
from an eighteenth century drawing by Revd J.R.P. Flinn
(Reproduced by permission of the *Dean & Chapter* of Kildare
Cathedral)

the goddess in the druid oak grove in the central plain of
Ireland, which later became the abbey of Kildare, went
on burning in Christian times. When the Welshman
Giraldus Cambrensis visited that place in the twelfth
century, he observed of the fire that he found there:

This they call inextinguishable, not that it could not be
extinguished, but because the nuns feed it with fuel and so
carefully that it has ever continued inextinct from the time
of the virgin [by which he meant the earthly Brigid] and
notwithstanding the great quantity of wood that has been
consumed during so long a time, yet the ashes have never
accumulated. When, in the time of Brigid, twenty nuns
served their Lord there, she made the twentieth. After her
glorious transit, nineteen always remained and the number
was not increased, and when each had kept the fire in order

in her own night, on the twentieth night the last nun put faggots on the fire, saying 'Brigid, keep your own fire, for the night has fallen to you.' And the fire being left so is found still burning in the morning. The fire is surrounded by a circular fence of twigs within which a male enters not, and if one should chance to presume to enter, which was sometimes attempted by giddy persons, he escaped not without enduring punishment. Also, it is permitted only for women to blow the fire, and for these, not with their own breath, but only with bellows or fans.

I feel that last restriction was important. The sacred fire had to be given life by the elemental air of the wind, and not through the breath that came from an individual woman's body. In the same way the spirit of Brigid is universal. It does not depend on any particular person. As for the fire, it was not until the dissolution of the abbey at the Reformation that the flames of Kildare were extinguished. The walls of the fire house itself remained on the hill by the abbey church until the eighteenth century and are recorded in drawings of that time. Now only the foundations remain.

It is fitting that in the Gaelic blessing on the *smooring*, the stacking of the peat fire to keep it smouldering until the morning, Brigid is invoked with Mary:

> I will smoor the hearth
> As Mary would smoor;
> The encompassment of Bride and of Mary
> On the fire and on the floor,
> And on the household all.

Two of the four elements were ascribed to Brigid, goddess and saint: the male element of fire and the female element of water. In the reverence paid to holy wells the rites of Brigid the goddess made a natural transition to the devotions made to the saint. As the guardian of childbirth and the spirit of fertility, both the goddess and the nun empowered the waters that were revered by women for many centuries. The involved rituals that took place at the holy wells and springs dedicated to Brigid, as young women came to ask a blessing on fruitful wombs and easy labours, are described in chapter 10.

Now I would like to return to the Brigid who was not only, or even especially, the guardian of women, but also the patron of poets, healers and craftsmen in metal. And, as we have seen, she had an additional role as the protector of cattle, in which all the wealth of a Celtic tribe depended. For hundreds of years crofters regarded her as 'Bride, tranquil of the kine', and in charms over the herds they sought her protection for their stock together with that of Columba:

> The protection of God and Columba
> Encompass your going and coming,
> And about you be the milkmaid of the smooth white palms,
> Brigid of the clustering hair, golden brown.

Although the writers who tell us of her life claim that Brigid was such a good milkmaid that her cows yielded three times a day, it is important to remember that her dairying has an allegorical side to it. If she is part of God's femininity, then in Jewish mystical thought she takes the place of Malkut, the kingdom of earth at the bottom of the ladder of the tree of the Kabbala. In such a place she is united to Tiferet the sphere of beauty and of the male principle of God, at the centre of the tree. This leads us back into the Indo-European inheritance of Celtic druidism. Brigid reminds us of the milkmaids who attended Krishna, but beyond that we also associate her with the nourishing cow itself, the archetypal image of the all-provider.

According to the Jewish Bible, the bride of the God of Israel can represent the earth itself. In Isaiah, 62, the prophet promises Zion that the land shall be married to Jehovah, 'For as a young man marrieth a virgin, so shall thy sons marry thee: and as the bridegroom rejoiceth over the bride, so shall thy God rejoice over thee.'

It is in this context that Brigid the earth mother is regarded as a provider, caring for the cattle in which the crofters' livelihoods depend. Yet she is more than that. She is a channel for the benevolence of nature and the mercy of God. It is in that role that she provides the means whereby men and women can reach the spiritual powers and, like the Virgin herself, her earthly form is pictured as ever young and ever fair.

The spirit of Brigid is part of an androgynous divinity, feeding the people with earthly food and with the milk of loving kindness. As an aspect of the feminine side of God, some words of Clement of Alexandria can relate to her: 'The Word is everything to the Child, both father and mother, teacher and nurse ... The nutrient is the milk of the father ... and only those who suck at this breast are truly happy. For this reason seeking is called sucking; to those infants who seek the Word, the Father's loving breasts supply milk.'

All these facts of Brigid the goddess come into the stories clustering round the life of the historical Brigid, who is said to have been born at Fochart near Dundalk on 1 February 450. Both the date and the year are important, for it was about that time that the reverberations of the teachings of Nestorius (which the Council of Ephesus attempted to quash on 7 June 431) must have reached these islands. The dispute at Ephesus centred on the role of Mary. From the third century she had occasionally been referred to as the Mother of God, a position that Nestorius challenged because he took the view that Mary did not bear God (was not in fact the God-bearer, the *Theotokos*, as many claimed her to be), but that she bore the man in whom the Word later became incarnate.

Nestorius was not only stating his position on the nature of Christ, he was also making it clear that he was anxious that Mary should not be given the status of a goddess. So at a time when the Virgin was being virtually dethroned as the Queen of Heaven, it was necessary for Brigid to emerge, almost to come to her assistance. Their names are frequently linked; moreover, Brigid was born at the time of Mary's feast of Candlemas, when the Candlemas bells (or snowdrops) carpet the druid oak groves and the days begin to lengthen. For the beginning of February is also the old Celtic feast of Imbolc, marking the time when the dark of winter begins to give way to the light of spring.

This timing, together with Brigid's association with fire, makes her above all a light bearer, embodying that aspect of the goddess which personifies the feminine urge to bring light and order to darkness and chaos. In actual terms this quality in a living women is shown in the sort of organizing ability that the abbess of a great monastic institution would have to exercise. It would also inform the practical benevolence that Brigid and her nuns were reputed to have shown as they worked among the poor, the sick and the dying.

This historical Brigid was the child of Dubtach, a prince of Leinster, and his maidservant, Broiccseach, neice of the holy Ultan of Ardbracan. Because of the jealousy shown by Dubtach's wife, Brigid and her mother were sold into slavery, serving the family of a druid priest. So she never knew an earthly home. Even her birth is said to have taken place on a threshold, neither within nor without a house. All these circumstances emphasize that as a baby Brigid had no fixed state or settled abode. Even as a child she was to belong more to the people and to the Church than to any human family.

Patrick, who may have baptized her, died when she

was only eight years old, but her biographers claim that before then she had established almost an adult relationship with Ireland's evangelizing saint. She used to tell him her dreams. In one of these she saw that 'the land was ploughed far and wide, and sowers went forth over it in white raiment. They sowed good seed, and it sprang up as a fair and abundant harvest. Then came the ploughers in black and sowers in black, and they hacked and tore up and destroyed the good wheat and sowed tares among it.' Patrick's sad interpretation of that vision was its foretelling of 'evil men and false teachers, who shall rise up after us and destroy us.'

Another dream that she had was more joyful. It foretold the birth of Columba, and in it she saw a northern sapling which grew into a great tree whose branches spread across Ireland and Scotland. Her place in time between Patrick and Columba, which is emphasized by the stories of these dreams, places her in the centre of Ireland's triad of great saints.

There was never any doubt that she belonged to the Church. Although she was brought up in a pagan household, her mother is said to have been Christian and no remarkable conversion stories are told of the young Brigid. At fourteen she resisted her father's attempt to make reparations to her by arranging a noble marriage. Instead she took the formal vows that were to make her a nun, and so embarked on the career which was to lead to the foundation of the abbey of Kildare. Great as she was to become, she never seems to have forgotten that she chose 'Blessed are the merciful' for her sign when she and the postulates who took their vows with her were asked to select the beatitude whose grace they most desired. The stories of her busy life are full of instances of her small acts of gentleness and mercy.

As abbess of Kildare Brigid ruled over a double monastery, a pattern familiar to the Celtic Church and practised in northern England over a century later, when

Ebba ruled Coldingham and Hilda was abbess of Whitby. In such institutions the monks could undertake the physical work that was beyond the powers of the women. They were also needed to serve as priests. For all its wisdom in many matters, the Celtic Church still held to the stricture of Tertullian, who would not permit a woman 'to teach, nor to baptize, nor to celebrate the Eucharist, nor to claim for herself a share in any masculine function – not to mention any priestly office.' These had to be performed by the monks, but in Brigid's case there was no question as to who ruled the abbey.

Brigid selected Conleath to be the bishop who would 'govern the church with her in episcopal dignity that nothing of the sacerdotal order might be wanting in her churches.' We note that the churches remained hers. Conleath died on 3 May 519, a few years before his abbess, and he was buried beneath the alter at Kildare.

When Brigid came to die, she was attended by one of her disciples, Nennidh, nicknamed the Clean Hand, because the saint had prophesied that when the time was ripe for her to journey out of this world he would give her the holy viaticum. It is told that she first met Nennidh when he was a young man racing in the Curragh, the wide grassy plain that lies to the east of Kildare, the place where the cream of the racehorses are given their training gallops now. When the nun stopped the lad in the midst of his athletics to ask him why he ran so fast, he gave her the flippant answer that he was in a hurry to get to Heaven. She decided to take him seriously and predicted that he would be a Christian priest.

Brigid was buried beside Conleath and her body lay at Kildare for three centuries. At the end of that time her remains were taken to lie beside those of Patrick at Downpatrick, in a shrine that was one of the most holy places in Ireland. As such it was despoiled at the Reformation and the relics were dispersed.

The reverence in which Brigid was held, however,

could not be so lightly destroyed. Perhaps it was at that time that the rush crosses of Brigid became common. These plaited crosses could easily have been dismantled or hidden in the face of Protestant persecution. That seems a practical explanation for the origin of these crosses, which are still made throughout Ireland, but folklore attributed the plaiting of the first one to Brigid herself. She is said to have made it as she worked to convert the druid family in which she and her mother were slaves.

Folklore had a more important part to play in linking Brigid to Mary on the earthly as well as the mystical plane. It was done by transforming her into the midwife and wet-nurse at the Nativity. Indeed, there is scriptural precedent for such a role. In chapter 14 of the apocryphal Protevangelum, Joseph seeks out a midwife to be present at Christ's birth.

In mystical terms there is no need to question how an Irish girl, born five centuries later, could have taken on this work in Bethlehem. Like Mary, Brigid goes beyond even the most nurturing of earthly mothers, who can only bring a child into a world in which he must eventually die. Mary (and by implication Brigid too) has the power as a spiritual mother to bear children into everlasting life. It was a doctrine propounded in Syriac literature in the fourth century by Ephrem, who wrote: 'The virgin earth of old gave birth to the Adam, who is lord of the earth, but today another Virgin has given birth to the Adam who is Lord of Heaven.' Ephrem also emphasized the perpetual wisdom of the Virgin by adhering to the tradition that Mary conceived the Word through her ear. And as the Eastern Church was to look on Sophia as embodying the wisdom of the Mother of God, so the Celts took Brigid as the life-preserving and enhancing feminine spirit who could grant the gift of immortality.

Certainly her cult spread far beyond Ireland. She is to

be found in place names and in church dedications in Scotland, Wales and England; and manuscript translations of the accounts of her life were made in French and German. Wherever the saints of the Irish Church wandered, they took the cult of Brigid with them.

Indeed, the widespread cult of Brigid is a reflection of the wandering spirit of the Irish monks. They seem to have taken the words of the second-century Bishop Iranaeus literally, when he defined the true search for God as starting from *aporia* (roadlessness), a state of complete trust in the direction of God rather than that of a human decision. In such a spirit they were to journey for God 'they cared not wither'; and as they went Brigid protected them.

7

The White Martyrdom

The Celts of the early Church were travellers of an especial sort. Occasional journeys could be interpreted as planned missionary projects; but often the instinct that motivated them to follow the example of Abraham and leave a settled homestead at God's command was even more compelling than the urge to spread the Gospel. Yet unlike the true itinerant who knows no home other than his boat or his tent, they had an intense nostalgic yearning (the *hiraeth* of the Welsh) for their homeland whenever they were away from it. This yearning was of an intensity only matched by the desire to be on their travels again once they were at home. It was a desperate sort of restlessness, not unknown to many people today, although they acted it out in a more extreme fashion than most of us are able to do. They had no refuge in safe tourism.

The wise Columba, who suffered his own exile from the oak groves of his beloved Derry, tried to bring some order and sense to those who longed to become wanderers for God. He told them that there were three kinds of travellers: the first leave their homeland with their spirit uncleansed, and so their travelling is purely physical and can serve no spiritual purpose; the second, being under authority to an institution, are only free to travel in spirit (Columba put such a restraint on some of his own monks when he felt that it was wise to do so); and the third group leave their country entirely, in both body and soul. Those are the travellers who have chosen to suffer the true white martyrdom of exile.

Unlike the red martyrdom, exile involves no deliberate spilling of blood; but it does imply a total renunciation of familar affections and securities and a bold stepping out into the unknown. The true *peregrinatus* did not journey in flight from despair or boredom; often he did not even go towards any definite goal. For him the journey was more important than the arrival, and often it was undertaken by water; sometimes, if we are to believe the hagiographies, in rudderless ships whose sails were set to take them wherever God's winds and tides would have them go. More than once, when Brendan's sails flapped idly for lack of wind and his monks no longer had the strength to row, he is reported to have encouraged them by saying, 'Brothers, do not fear. God is our helper, sailor and helmsman, and He guides us. Ship all the oars and the rudder. Just leave the sails spread and God will do as he wishes with His servants and their ship.'

Those hypothetical words may not ring completely false, but they do have the sound of a last resort. In most normal circumstances I am certain that the leaders of these voyages would not abandon the God-given gift of common sense and allow their frail craft to be dashed to pieces on the rocks for want of a hand on the helm. Certainly they enjoyed the challenge of danger, but when Columba dared the wicked whirlpool of Corryvrechan to the north of Jura, one can be sure that he took full account of tides and currents.

There are two aspects to these sea journeys. They can be interpreted as allegories or as history. Both aspects are important. In recounting the stories of the voyages of the saints the chroniclers were often making a Christianized version of the Old Irish *imram*, a tale of mythological travel. The best-known, lengthiest and most detailed examples of such a form are the many versions of the often told tale of the westward voyages of Brendan to seek the Island of the Blest, first written down in Latin in Ireland during the ninth century and most recently broadcast in 1984 as a radio verse play by the Orkney poet George Mackay Brown. In both these accounts Brendan's adventures, which include an encounter with a whale which his crew mistook for an island and the discovery of a charmed well that had a soporific effect on all who drank from it, are more reminiscent of the trials of Ulysees on his return from Troy or those recounted in the early seventh-century *Voyage of Bran* than of any geographical description of an actual journey however far-fetched.

We can read the accounts of the astonishing journeys of the saints in much the same way as the Gnostics approached the Scriptures. I do not think that even the most gullible ever took these stories literally. What we have here is a set of tales that can be relished in their own right or taken as moral allegories by thse who have a taste for such charades. Beyond the ethical interpretation they provide charts for the spiritual journeys which can be undertaken in this life, and which must be embarked on at death when the soul finds itself in unknown territory. Less subtle and detailed than the Egyptian and the Tibetan Books of the Dead, these tales respond to the need that we all feel to envisage the ultimate journey into the unknown. For in all cultures there is the expectation that the soul's immediate experience, after mind and body no longer hold it to the physical world, will be that of a traveller.

Such a metaphysical journey must have seemed very close to the men and women of the Celtic Church who set out to cross the sea in frail coracles or in skin-covered long boats. We know of at least two shipwrecks recorded in the laconic Iona annals. They took place in

the mid-seventh century, presumably in the turbulent
waters that separate the island of Mull from the
mainland. If lives could be lost on such short crossings,
the saints who set out to cross oceans must always have
been prepared for disaster.

Woodcut from *Sankt Brandans Seefahrt*, Augsburg, *1476*
(reproduced by permission of Doliven Press Ltd. from *The
Voyage of Saint Brendan* John J. O'Meara trans.)

Yet hazardous as their voyages were, the Celts who
sailed up and down Europe's Atlantic seaboard from
Ireland to Spain were following the routes taken by
many generations of adventurous traders who brought
their craft north from the Mediterranean. It is the more
remarkable when the saints ventured into the unknown
north, as they surely did, for, according to the
geographer Dicuil, an Irish scholar in the Carolingian
court, there were Irish settlers in the Faroes and Iceland
by the end of the eighth century.

Two hundred years before that Columba's friend
Cormac is reported to have sailed beyond the Orkneys in
his desire to 'find a desert place in the sea that cannot be

crossed'. Such an intrepid sailor probably came of a great line of navigators. Columba's royal ancestor, Niall of the Nine Hostages, was a sea pirate, whose raiders could have well been involved in the kidnap of a sixteen-year-old Romano-Briton from the shores of the Solway Firth and so have been instrumental in bringing Patrick to Ireland. That missionary saint's journey were altogether more orderly and nearer home than those of the leaders of the Church who grew up in his adopted land. Still it was no mean adventure to take a curragh, as he did, from Mayo beach to Cahar island between Clare and Inishturk. His seamen were well enough regarded for the Inchagoill grave of his nephew and pilot-navigator Lugnaid to have been marked by an inscribed stone shaped like a rudder and rudder plate.

Lugnaid's contemporaries and his crew were mostly island crofter-fishermen with a great respect for the vast waters and for those who sailed them. It is only reasonable to imagine that many sailors set out then, as they do now, in a spirit of adventure and exploration, and that many of the missionary expeditions and the penitential aspects of leaving the comforts of home were merely excuses for a voyage of inquiry. No doubt many a monk who set out from his homeland was guilty of Columba's charge of journeying in body only.

We cannot be sure of that, but at least we know something of the kind of craft that they set out in. The present-day Clare curragh probably gives us a fair model of all those in use along the west coast of Ireland. It is a long boat covered by canvas, stretched over a frame, which is then given two coats of boiling tar. The craft was propelled by bladeless oars. The ninth-century life of Brendan tells how he used iron tools to build a wooden boat, which he covered with ox hides tanned with oak bark. He then smeared the outside joints with fat, and all was done according to the methods which the narrator says was customary in his time and country.

It is ironic that all this Irish voyaging, and the Christianity that largely motivated it, should have been brought to an end by crueller and more determined sea raiders than the pagan Celts had ever been. When the Vikings swooped round the northern coast of Scotland to plunder the Irish settlements, few dared meet them on the waves. The great thalassocracy of Europe's Atlantic seaboard was overturned from the east.

Long before that happened the Celtic saints had not only crossed the seas they had also made land journeys remarkable in the conditions prevailing in the disintegration of the elaborate communications of the Roman Empire. In the fifth century Ninian who had gone over the Alps to Rome, went on to Tours to visit the White House of Martin before he returned to his native Galloway. In Gaul he experienced the sort of monastic settlement that inspired him to set up his own Candida Casa on the Solway Firth. In north Britain his missionary journeys to convert the Picts took him through wolf-infested forests and the mountain passes of Scotland from southwest to northeast, and some say even across the northern sea to Shetland.

A hundred years later the Irish Columbanus, whose life was written by a monk and fellow countryman of the mid-seventh century, set out from Bangor in his homeland with twelve companions. He was about forty years old when he arrived in France in 585. Then for twenty years he settled in the ruined Roman fortress of Annegray in the Vosges mountains, adhering to the customs of the Celtic Church and keeping Easter according to the Irish calculations. For that, and because of his vociferous objections to an administration which gave bishops supremacy over abbots, he was persecuted by the Gaulish Church to such an extent that he went south into Italy, arriving near Milan in 612. A year later he settled at Bobbio, founding a monastery on the site of a ruined church and, despite his age, adding his own labours to the work of reconstructing the buildings.

Journeys such as Columbanus made, partly under-taken in response to political pressure, were made on a smaller scale by the hundreds of Celtic monks who sailed from Wales across the Severn Sea to land on the north coast of the southwest peninsula. Some of these Irish and Welsh saints, like Petroc, who came from South Wales to land at the mouth of the River Hayle and become the patron saint of Cornwall, never crossed water again. Among the settlers in Cornwall were the holy women often referred to as the daughters of Brychan, a legendary Welsh king of Brecon. It is likely that these women were not blood sisters, but that they originally belonged to some monastic settlement which had been granted land by a tribe claiming Brychan as ancestor. The women are real enough. There is Morwenna, who gave her name to Morwenstow, and Endelion, who also has a place named after her in Cornwall, as does their 'sister' Mabyn. Farther east, near the mouth of the Severn, Brigid herself is supposed to have landed. I find that difficult to believe. There is certainly a church dedicted to her at Berrow, a little to the west of the natural harbour formed by the headland of Brean Down which stretches into the Bristol Channel from Weston-super-Mare, and her cult was certainly observed in Glastonbury, where a group of outlying fields still bear the name of Bride's Meadows. Yet I do not think that the abbess of Kildare came through Wales to cross the Severn Sea, but maybe one of her nuns did make that journey.

Possibly a whole group of Brigid's nuns came into Somerset, for often a saint like Columbanus took companions on his journey. Petroc took twelve monks when he left the monastery of Bodmin to live on the wild moor to the east; and we can imagine the women would have also travelled as a group. Similar bands of companions ventured even farther into the unknown,

leaving Cornwall to cross the sea to Gaul. Companionship on a journey is another motivation for travel, a
valuable byproduct of the main purpose in that it binds
people more closely together as they share the hazards of
the journey and the insecurity of unfamiliar places.
When they came to make new settlements, the leaders
would be glad of a nucleus of followers related by a
common experience. And when they reached the island-
strewn coast of Brittany, the Roman Amorica, which
was to become colonized by Celtic Britons, they made
many such settlements. The places they chose can easily
be recognized by the prefixes *plou, loo, tref,* which have
affinites to the Cornish *tre,* and *lann* like the Welsh *llan.*

Besides these geographical prefixes, which all relate
to a settlement or stretch of land, there are many
parallels in church dedications between Cornwall and
Brittany; but most striking of all is the similarity
between the two St Michael's Mounts which face the sea
on either side of the Channel. Here one feels strongly
that Michael the Archangel is recalled in his aspect of
Mannon, god of the sea, a protector and navigator for the
men who risked their lives on the crossing.

Some of these men were bound past the treacherous
currents of Ushant and across the Bay of Biscay to
northern Spain. There was a Celtic monastery at Sancta
Maria de Bretõa near Mondenedo in Galicia, which was
destroyed in the Arab conquest of the seventh century.
The links with Ireland go back long before that, for a
fifth-century Spanish document tells of a settlement in
the region called Brigantia, which was in some way
connected with Brigid the goddess.

Three explanations have been given for these southern
migrations. The journeys may have been taken purely as
missionary ventures, and certainly the paths of the saints
are marked by the monastic settlements which they
founded wherever they stayed for any length of time. On
the other hand, the Welsh monks seem to have had two

valid reasons for leaving their homeland. It has been suggested that they found themselves pincered between an influx of Irish invaders and raiders on the Welsh coast, from the Lleyn peninsula to St David's Head, and the Saxon hordes coming in from the east. About the same time they would have been anxious to flee from the virulent outbreaks of yellow plague, a form of hepatitis, that hit the country in the fifth and sixth centuries.

Probably all these conjectures hold good in some measure. Certainly the missionary purpose cannot be entirely discounted, although Amorica was Christian before the Britons arrived and had its own missionary sees at Nantes, Rennes and Vannes. Nora Chadwick has shown that the Welsh saints, or learned men, were not so much evangelists as leaders of a migration. However, there is no denying that once they had crossed the Channel they established a church on the Irish pattern, and their hagiographers certainly wanted to express their missionary intent. The legends bear this out. It is remarkable how many of the men and women who crossed the sea from Wales are supposed to have done so on a floating stone. We have already seen that the druids held a floating stone to be possessed of miraculous healing powers, but the saints' stones probably represented a portable altar such as the Celtic monks always took with them on their travels.

A less easily explained druidic element also comes into the legends of their journeys. Wherever the saints landed you can still find a well dedicated to their memory and, as in the instance of Decuman in the Somerset port of Watchet, the well often has a story based on the severed-head cult of the druids, who believed that the whole essence of a person existed in the head. This aspect of the Celtic travels is examined more closely in chapter 10.

Despite the legends there is no doubt that the wells are real markers of landing places, for one of the most desperate needs of any sea traveller is a source of fresh

water. There are many little inlets on the coast of
Brittany where the Welsh Samson is supposed to have
landed, but it is one on the edge of Finistère, on the
headland above the low cliffs of the rocky shore near
Ploudalmezau, which seems the most authentic to me.
The place is still marked by an ancient cross and a
carefully covered well and, despite the holiday cottages
in the background, the coast still retains something of the
wild desolation that Samson and his followers must have
encountered.

From that well he went east to establish his main
monastery at Dol, and as he went he and his monks
probably inscribed the tall prehistoric menhirs they
encountered with the Christian symbols that still mark
them today. These Welshmen certainly forged such
strong linguistic links with Brittany that the language of
Breton, Welsh and Cornish retained similarities for
many centuries. The Welsh cattle drovers who settled as
milkmen in London in the last century found themselves
conversing fairly easily with the Breton onion sellers,
and there is a strong similarity between the folk music of
Brittany and Wales.

The Irish and Welsh monks influenced the Bretons in
other ways besides that of language. From the life of
Columbanus we know that the Celts angered the Roman
Church in Gaul by insisting on their own customs and
organization, which gave the abbots supremacy over the
bishops. Indeed, it was not until the ninth century that
Charlemagne managed to substitute the Roman territorial for the Celtic monastic bishoprics throughout
Brittany.

As far back as the early sixth century Melaine, Bishop
of Rennes, wrote to the Breton priests of the Celtic
Church telling them to renounce the habit of 'wandering
from cabin to cabin celebrating Mass on portable altars,
accompanied by women administering the chalice to the
faithful.' Evidently the monks from Britain brought the

practice of double monasteries with them, and felt free to involve the women in priestly functions in ways that had not been usual at home.

Although the established Church was to gain supremacy in Brittany, in one respect it failed to exercise its authority. The Irish Church always insisted on a form of penance that was part of confession, part pilgrimage, and this has lived on in the form of the Breton *pardonnes*. In some ways these processions, festive despite the funereal chanting, reflect the Celtic urge to wander. They depend on movement. Although some sort of sacramental walk is common to almost all cultures and religions, these penitential journeys can best be understood in the light of Hindu practice, and as such the tradition may have influenced the Indo-European druids, who passed it on to the Celtic Church.

The Hindus believe that at some stage in life one should make a penance for the sin of attachment to and greed for material things by casting them off and setting out from home with only the barest necessities for a virtually unplanned journey. If this is not sufficient to enable a person to extinguish greed and anger and to realize the illusion of desire, then more severe forms of deprivation are indicated, such as walking barefoot, or, in extreme conditions, on the knees, so that all else but discomfort is forgotten.

The attitude in which the Celtic saints set out, leaving friends and homeland in order to journey for God, is certainly similar to that of the Hindu penitent. That such a similarity was intended (even though the Hindu source must have been unrealized) is apparent in the tradition that Columba left Ireland in penitence for bringing about the slaughter of the Battle of Culdreimhne, supposedly caused by his refusal to give up a psalter which he had copied.

Columba's penitence was so extreme that he vowed he would not settle in any place from which it was possible to look across the sea to his beloved homeland. It was because of that vow that he came to found his monastery at Iona, and the end of his journey was in that respect similar to those of the monks and nuns who made the sea journey from Wales to Cornwall and Brittany, and also to those of the more modest travellers who wandered over the countryside with small bands of followers, eventually settling down in a group of beehive cells round a water source and building a small wattle and daub oratory adorned with a wooden cross.

Some of these little settlements were to grow into great monastic colleges, but the travellers who founded them often retained the urge to travel on alone. When, through age and circumstance, long physical journeys became inappropriate, they retired to a solitary place to embark on the hazards of an inner spiritual journey. So after establishing his monastery at Bobbio, Columbanus went to die in a cave on a mountainside. And his pupil Gall, who founded an abbey in the heart of the Swiss Alps, refused the position of abbot, living out his days as a hermit and occasional itinerant preacher.

PART THREE

Places

8

The Desert

Our word 'hermit' comes from the Greek *eremites* – dwellers in the desert – and it is from the Egyptian desert that the Celtic fathers inherited the practice of living solitary lives in remote places, where isolation was increased by inaccessibility. To understand their motivation we must go back to the third century and the account of the life of Paul, who may have been a fictitious figure, an amalgam of all the early hermits that his biographer, Jerome, had ever heard of. Certainly Paul's prototypes existed, for by the time that his life was written in the fourth century many solitaries were out in the desert, living lives of extreme asceticism, following the example of Paul's younger contemporary, the historical Antony, whose life was written by Athanasius in 357.

Athanasius addressed that *Vita* to the *peregrinos frates*, assuring those wandering brothers that 'The rivalry you have entered into with the Egyptian monks is excellent, determined as you are to equal or even surpass them.' It is certain that members of the Celtic Church were among those wanderers, and that their immediate descendants would also read the *Lausaiac History*, a popular work written by Palladius at the beginning of the fifth century and comprising a collection of anecdotes about the desert hermits. Palladius told of women solitaries as well as men, and it is through him that we know of Alexandria, a maidservant, who left the city to spend ten years in a tomb-like dwelling, during which time she never looked at anybody face to face. When the Abbess Melania asked her how she managed to endure being so isolated, and how she dealt with attacks of accidie or despair induced by her situation, she gave a detailed account of how her days were spent: 'From early morning to the ninth hour I pray hour by hour, spinning flax the while. During the remaining hours I meditate on the holy patriarchs and prophets and apostles and martyrs. And having eaten my bread I remain in patience for the other hours, waiting for my end with cheerful hope.'

Alexandria's self-confessed cheerfulness is in marked contrast to the almost aggressive misery of some of her contemporary solitaries whose remarks are quoted in chapter 3. Nevertheless, Alexandria was quite orthodox in counting *accidie* among the deadly sins, and she may well have been able to find herself in agreement with those Tibetian Buddhists who claim that the greatest courage is the courage to be happy. That is an outlook that has survived among solitaries through the centuries. In the 1930s an Anglican nun, Sister Adeline Cashmore, lived as a solitary for four years on the northern slopes of the Mendip Hills. Her confessor described her as 'one of the merriest people I ever knew'.

The leaders of the Irish Church in the fifth and sixth centuries had another great work to put beside Palladius' anecdotes, for his teacher Evagrius wrote out of his own experience of the spirit that motivated the desert hermits. When Evagrius came from the Holy Land to Egypt in the middle of the fourth century, like many another traveller he went to ask one of the abbas, possibly the great Macarius of Scete, to give him a word to live by: 'Tell me some piece of advice by which I may be able to save my soul,' he begged, and was told, 'If you wish to save your soul you should not speak before you are asked a question.'

Fortunately for us Evagrius did continue to speak or at any rate to write, and the almost Zen-like quality of that encounter is echoed in much of his work. At least two twentieth-century writers – H. U. von Balthasar and Thomas Merton – have claimed* that in many ways his theology of prayer was closer to Buddhism than to Christianity. So perhaps it is not surprising that this disciple of Origen should have been listed as a heretic by Rome during the sixth century and declared anathema on account of his Gnosticism, his belief in the existence of the soul before birth, and his doctrine of the absolute immaterialism of God.

However much the orthodox Church of the sixth century may have shied away from Evagrius' teaching, it seems reasonable to believe that his books, and especially those which are concerned with prayer and contemplation (the chief work of the hermit), reflect the practice of the desert fathers. He recommended a hesychia born of solitude, an interior eremitism which reflects the emptiness of the hermit's cave. Upon such silence rested the Christian *apatheia*, which resembles the non-attachment of the Buddhist, and which alone can nourish the feeling of *agape*, the state of universal love and peace to all beings and the key that turns the despair of loneliness into a positive solitude.

The chief enemy of such a state, and the cause of all distraction, is anger. In his *Chapters on Prayer* Evagrius tell us: 'No one who loves true prayer and yet gives way to anger or resentment can be absolved from the imputation of madness, for he resembles a man who desires to see clearly and for that purpose he scratches his eyes.'

The demons of anger often took a physical form for the solitaries. From the sixth and seventh centuries, by which time the leaders of the Celtic Church were leaving their settlements to live alone in wild places,

*H. U. von Balthasar *Zeitscrift fur fak Aszeze und Mystik*, 1939; Thomas Merton *Zen and the Birds of Appetite*, 1968.

come many accounts of torments by hordes of demons. It was an accepted hazard, a risk to be taken by those who isolated themselves from their fellows; and it can be explained by the psychological fact that, as the natural projections onto other people are necessarily withdrawn, they take on a more dangerous and sinister form before they can finally be dissolved.

Seen in that light, it is obvious that the hermit's withdrawal is not a flight or escape from the difficulties of life. Samuel Johnson's remark that whenever he read of a hermit he kissed his feet in imagination seems to me to be a valid response, at any rate to the solitaries of the early Church. They were not recluses cut off from the misery around them. They withdrew from the business of the world in order to confront its suffering. Their prayers were designed to help other people, and in particular they were concerned with the lot of travellers, both in the spiritual and the physical sense. It was a tradition which persisted. During the 1930s Sister Mary Fidelia, a clergyman's daughter who lived alone in a cottage belonging to the House of St Francis at Ffestiniog in North Wales, dedicated herself to praying for wayfarers.

In the Middle Ages hermits were often required to take charge of the repairs of roads and bridges, to ferry travellers across rivers, and to provide overnight food and shelter. Indeed, the laws of hospitality were paramount and were respected by the hermit as strenuously as by any other desert dweller. In Britain, where many hermits were expected to be as self-sufficient as Cuthbert was on the island of Inner Farne, small guesthouses were provided for those travellers who came to seek advice and consolation. No one was turned away without food and drink, although the hermit could be sparing of his words to anybody who had come to see him purely out of curiosity.

All hermits, however, would be prepared to spend a

The Man symbol of St. Matthew. Gospel of St. Matthew.
Book of Kells.

Guthlac receiving his tonsure, from *The Legendary History of St. Guthlac* by Richard Gough. (pub. 1815) (Reproduced by permission of the British Library.)

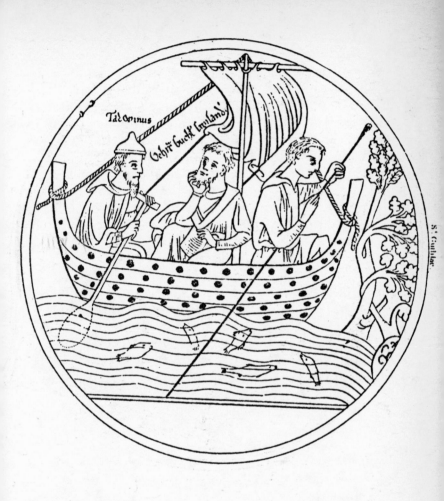

St Guthlac from *The Legendary History of St Guthlac* by Richard
Gough (pub. 1815) (reproduced by permission of the British
Library.)

whole night talking with those who sought them out as soul friends and sources of comfort and inspiration. Athanasius described Antony as 'a physician given by God to Egypt' and tells us that many people from all parts of the Roman Empire took long journeys to seek the hermit's help. Antony himself made it clear why a solitary should be in a position to help others, explaining that 'he who knows himself knows God: and he who knows God knows also the dispensations which he makes for his creatures.'

The hermits' advice was sought in response to political as well as to personal problems. Bede tells us that when the bishops of the Celtic Church were perplexed as to how they should welcome Rome's envoy Augustus, a hermit or anchorite attached to the Welsh monastery at Bangor told them to make the test of humility. If Augustus was like Christ in regarding himself as the servant of all, then he would surely stand when the bishops approached. If he behaved in that way, he could be trusted as a worthy leader. So that the matter could be clearly tested, the Celtic bishops arranged to come late to the planned meeting at the source of the Thames where the land of the West Saxons met that of the Celtic Hwiccas. When they arrived Augustus remained seated, as the wise hermit probably knew he would. So the divergence between the Celtic and the Roman Churches hardened.

Although that divergence was to end officially with defeat of the Celtic Church at Whitby, the practice of the eremetic life did not end then. Cuthbert went to Inner Farne for the first time in 675, and it was in August 699 that Guthlac, then only twenty-six years old, took a boat across the waters that divided the swampy islands of the Cambridgeshire fens and settled by a Roman barrow at Croyland, literally a 'crude or muddy land'. The wasteland to which he came was just as desolate as Cuthbert's storm-girt island or the cave on the rocky

shore of the north coast of the Solway Firth in which
Ninian spent hours of solitary prayer.

Guthlac's life, written some fifty years after the
saint's death, tells us that when he went to Croyland he
deliberately chose 'a place which many men had
attempted to inhabit, but in which no man could settle
on account of manifold horrors and fears, and the
loneliness of the wide wilderness.' He had been warned
about it by Tatwine, the boatman from Ely who took
him to the place, who told him that no one could inhabit
the isle of Croyland 'by reason of strange apparitions
and devils appearing there'.

When the antiquarian William Stukeley, who was to
become the rector of nearby Stamford, first visited
Croyland in 1708, he found that it was still a wild and
lonely area 'scituate in the midst of a fenny, boggy level,
in winter time impassable by the overflowing of the
waters coming from the high countries and not having
passage to the sea.'

Although Guthlac was accompanied by both Tatwine
and Cissa, a wealthy convert, both of whom were to join
him in his hermitage, he did not escape the onslaught of
demons when he settled in this desolate morass.
According to an Anglo-Saxon poem on his life, a whole
'death-might' of cursed devils banded together against
him, and only through the most resolute courage was he
able to hold his ground. These horrible creatures had
great heads, long necks, faces adorned with filthy,
matted beards, distorted expressions, fierce eyes, foul
mouths, and their teeth were like those of horses.
Furthermore their throats were filled with flame, their
voices grated and shrieked, and they stood uneasily on
crooked legs with great swollen joints.

Perhaps Guthlac and his wretched companions,
sickened with deprivation, ill with fever, hungry,
thirsty, unwashed and frustrated by solitude and
discomfort, were simply catching sight of their own

reflections in the swampy waters. If that was so, then Guthlac dealt with the situation wisely. When these devils tried to egg him on to make even more inordinate fasts, so that he would be held the more firmly in their clutches, he sent them away and insisted on taking food in moderate quantities. In that temperance he was following Palladius' dictum that 'Drinking wine with reason is better far than drinking water in arrogance.'

The devils that Guthlac conjured up must have had something of the same nature as those demons who came to torment the dying Cuthbert as he lay for five days alone on Inner Farne, cut off from the mainland and from the monks on Lindisfarne by tumultuous seas. He had nothing to eat but five raw onions, and when his friends were at last able to come to him, he told them that his adversaries had persecuted him more harshly during the last week of his life than they had done in all the years that he had spent as a solitary.

If Guthlac's and Cuthbert's courage was so tested, it is not surprising that the Church leaders felt that some sort of preparation was essential for those who wished to lead a solitary life. In his writings on the Egyptian solitaries Evagrius made it clear that anyone living alone had to be prepared for attacks by demons. He explained that, in a community, people are always being indirectly attacked through the annoyance caused by their companions and by the tensions of communal life, but that in the desert demons can no longer use human intermediaries and so they make direct attacks. However infuriating our companions may be, as Evagrius warned his readers, they are infinitely easier to contend with than an encounter with demons; and as demons are more terrible than people, so the solitary life is much more dangerous than life in a community.

We have already seen how a modern psychologist would interpret Evagrius' words, and he would surely agree with that Church father in warning people that any encounter with our own negative forces can be dangerous and should be prepared for, and that anyone who is either overgregarious or seriously withdrawn will be at a particular risk. These dangers were all appreciated in the sixth century, and we know from a letter that Columbanus wrote to the Pope that Gildas had been consulted by the Irish Finnian on the vexed question of the troubles caused by inadequately trained monks and nuns setting out to live as hermits, inspired only by a zeal for the ascetic and solitary life and with no adequate understanding of what it involved.

Gildas knew what he was talking of. A married man, who did not enter a monastery until his late middle age when his children were grown up, he is supposed to have spent some solitary months on the tiny island of Steep Holm in the Bristol Channel; and when he came to settle for a while with the community around the wattle church at Glastonbury, he would go from time to time to live alone by the banks of the inland lake formed by the river Brue at that time. There he made his hermitage on the piece of high ground on which Street's parish church was to be built. And when he went to Brittany he resumed a solitary life, living as a hermit on the Ile d'Houat, until he was conceded territory on the mainland on which he could build his monastery.

Eventually it was to become canon law that no monk or nun was to be allowed to live as a hermit without preliminary monastic training in contemplation. So although historically the practice of hermitage was established in Egypt before monasteries were formed, in the West it was the general practice for those who wished to lead a solitary life to spend some time in a monastic settlement beforehand. Indeed, most of the hermits whose names have come down to us were themselves founders of monastic settlements but, following the example of Martin at Marmoutier, lived alone at some distance from the parent monastery. In this way they hoped to combine their pastoral duties with long stretches of solitary prayer.

It was an example that was followed throughout the centuries. In the wooded cliffs some 30 feet above the lower lake of Glendalough in the Wicklow hills there is a man-made cave cut into the rock. Its inner chamber is about 4 feet wide and 3 feet high, and it is approached by a short passageway of the same height and of almost half the width. It was probably made as a shelter long before Kevin founded his monastery in the valley; none the less the tradition that makes this cave the saint's sleeping place may well be founded on fact. To the east of the cave was his cell, mentioned in one of the early accounts of his life as being a place set among trees on a spur of rock overlooking the lake.

The remains of this beehive cell, in which Kevin spent four solitary years, can still be found. The steps up which the saint climbed to his fastness are still visible among the rocks of the hillside, although the present path follows an easier ascent through a clearing in the trees. The spur of rock is a flat ledge, and on it the circumference of the cells is marked out by a ring of stones.

As Kevin retreated from the communities he had inspired, so Columba sometimes left the cares of Iona and sailed to Hinba, an island which most scholars take to be one of the remote Garvellachs; and when Petroc took a band of followers into the wastes of Bodmin Moor, he established them in a group of huts on Rough Tor, left them there and walked a mile or two to the south, to live alone on Roughtor Marsh. Here, where a solitary ruined farmhouse stands on a little ridge of high ground above the boggy valley, is a small, round, corbelled hut, which many people claim is Petroc's cell. Whether that is so or not, and whether the building is simply a medieval pigsty or outbuilding as the cynical suggest, there is no doubt that in some such dwelling the saint lived, having ousted the previous hermit on the moor. Apart from his name, Gorran, we know little of the latter save that his need to be solitary was so great that, rather than stay anywhere near Petroc's monks, he moved southwards, perhaps even crossing the sea to Brittany.

The cell on Bodmin Moor is only one of many places in Britain which mark the site of a Celtic hermitage. Many inland caves, like the one above the village of Weem to the north of Aberfeldy, inhabited for a while by the young Cuthbert, carry legends of hermit occupation. Along the coast there are other caves which bear even clearer witness to the men who lived in them and to the pilgrims who venerated the site. At Ellary, in a bay of the sea loch of Caolisport in north Kintyre, there is a cave in which it is claimed Columba may have sheltered. Whether he did or not, it was certainly a holy place. The stone altar on its eastern wall is still in place and there is a cross carved in the rock above it. Other more elaborate crosses are cut into the rocks at the entrance to Ninian's Cave in Galloway, which faces south across the Solway Firth to the Isle of Man.

In summer that cave is an attractive place. Bleak as the rocky shore is here, a stream flows through it to the sea, providing an essential supply of fresh water. A little way inland its banks are alight with yellow flags, red campion and brilliant pink thrift. But in the gales of autumn and winter the coast is desolate, frightening even, and Ninian and the hermits who followed him to the cave must have often been cut off from human contact, although the place is no more than an hour's brisk walk from Whithorn.

The hermits who settled on islands took an even more serious risk of enduring long periods of total isolation, even if, like Cuthbert's friend Herbert, they settled for inland lakes, as he did with Derwent Water. The eighth-century Baldred, who lived alone on the Bass

St. Kevin's Cell. The remains of the cell overlooking the upper lake.

from *Glendalough* by Kenneth MacGowan. Drawing by Muriel O'Connor, reproduced by permission of Kamac Publications, Dublin.

Rock by New Berwick on the Firth of Forth, is said to have actually caused the reef now known as St Baldred's Rock to be removed to its present position. Originally it had stood between the rock and the mainland and made the crossing doubly hazardous. Other hermits more determined on isolation found sanctuary on tiny Hebridean islands off the coast of Lewis or so far out into the Atlantic that access was almost totally impossible for most of the year, although I think we may discount the legend that there was ever a hermit on Rockall. In such cases it is the archaeologists rather than the hagiographers and the folklorists who can decide if these bare rocks were once inhabited.

Of the island hermitages, the holy island of Bardsey at the western tip of the Lleyn peninsula is the most renowned. Separated from the mainland by the wild waters of seven tides and their attendant currents, the

The chancel arch and interior of the Reefert Church

from *Glendalough* by Kenneth MacGowan. Drawing by Muriel O'Connor, reproduced by permission of Kamac Publications, Dublin.

island is still a place of hermitage. The Anglican sister who lives there has only the lighthouse keepers for neighbours and, although the island is only 4 or 5 miles from the little port of Aberdarn, it is often inaccessible for months and anyone who visits it, even in summer, must be prepared to be storm-stayed for days. Only the presence of the manned lighthouse brings the sister's isolation into bounds that our society can tolerate.

She belongs to an order which has other solitaries living on the Welsh mainland in separate caravans and cottages. This grouping of hermits follows the Egyptian pattern at Cellia, some 50 miles south of Alexandria, where a group of austere hermit monks lived their separate lives. It was from such groupings that the first monasteries were formed. So as monastic settlements gathered round hermitages, they in turn formed the training grounds in which a new generation of dedicated solitaries could be prepared for the eremetic life. It is clear at Croyland, where, as we have seen, Guthlac settled with Cissa and Tatwine, his boatman, and where he was later joined by his sister Pega. There is a familiar element in the legend which tells that Guthlac was led to the precise site of his settlement by the spirit which told him to make his hermitage at a place where he should find a sow suckling her piglets. There he found water. Felix, Guthlac's eighth-century biographer, describes that site as 'a great mound raised upon the earth; which same, of yore, men had dug and broken up in the hopes of finding treasure. On the other side of the mound a place was dug, as it were a great water cistern. Over this cistern, the blessed man Guthlac built himself a house at the beginning, as soon as he settled himself in the hermit station.'

Guthlac's well is still visible in the south wall of Croyland Abbey. A mile or so the east is the present-day village of Peakirk, where Pega had her cell, on an artificial platform raised above the fens. Here a cross shaft has been discovered and it is displayed in the modern chapel on the site. It has interlacing foliage carved around its stem, so linking its Christian symbolism with the Norse Yggdrasil in a way that is reminiscent of the Ruthwell cross.

There was a chantry at Pega's hermitage throughout the Middle Ages, and although the chapel fell into disuse after the Dissolution, it was restored during the nineteenth century. For the last fifty years a group of Anglican nuns have lived in a specially built house of prayer beside it. The first nuns to be housed there belonged to a teaching order, and that would have pleased Stukeley. When he was rector of Stamford he visited the site on 6 July 1757 and noted that Guthlac's and Pega's cells were 'the spring-head and seminary of all our learning; the source of the two universities of Cambridge and Stamford.' He obviously could not quite get over the fact that Stamford's serious claim to be England's second university city had been usurped.

— 9 —

Monasteries

The great monastic schools of the Celtic Church were the flowering of a combination of the inheritance from the druidical colleges and the coenobitic movement in the Egyptian desert. The lives of the saints are full of accounts of men who went into the monastic schools in Wales or Ireland for a period of twenty years, the length of time taken to train a druid priest. And, no doubt, much of the training, in so far as it involved the commitment of long passages to memory, was similar. Furthermore many British monasteries were actually founded on sites of druid colleges.

However, the idea of a Christian monastic community came from Egypt. The first Christian community in which several hundred men and women joined together to live apart from the secular world was set up in Tabennesi in southern Egypt in 318. That institution was founded by Pachomius, a Christian convert who had served in Constantine's army. Our information about Tabennesi comes from Palladius, who found the Greek translation of a Coptic document concerning it in Nitria. This text, from which he quotes in his *Lausiac History*, tells of the vision which inspired Pachomius to set up his monastery.

When the convert was living in a cave as a hermit, he saw an angel who said, 'So far as you are concerned, you

conduct your life perfectly. It is vain for you to continue
sitting in your cave! Come now, leave this place and go
out and call the young monks together. Rule them by the
model which I am now going to give you.' The angel
then instructed him to arrange separate cells in a cloister,
with space in each cell for three monks. Meals could be
taken in common, but any monk who desired to be more
solitary could eat bread and salt in his cell. The monks
were to be arranged in twenty-four groups, each group
being assigned a letter of the Greek alphabet which had a
spiritual significance known only to the initiates.

As the monastic movement spread beyond Tabennesi,
Pachomius decreed that each monastery founded as part
of his order should be surrounded by a wall, and that it
should contain a church, a general meeting place, a
refectory and a library, as well as a storeroom for
clothes, a kitchen, a larder, a bakery, an infirmary and
craftsmen's shops with space for a blacksmith, a tanner, a
carpenter, a fuller and a cobbler. At this time, when
there were between 5000 and 7000 monks in the Thebaid,
each monastery could contain 1440 monks grouped in ten
equal tribes each of which was further divided into four
houses.

These highly organized communities seem far removed from the earlier cluster of hermits' cells, yet there
were many similarities. Like the hermits, the communities of monks divided their days into periods of prayer,
manual work and study, in which they included the
labour of transcription, as well as work in the fields and
the domestic duties concerned with the running of the
monastery. Of all these activities, prayer was the most
important and formed the main reason for their
existence. The formal times of communal prayer took
place at dawn, midday and sundown. In addition, six
prayers were recited before retiring and there was a
further service at midnight. Mass was held on Saturdays,
Sundays and holy days, and the abbot gave spiritual

instruction twice a week during fasts as well as on Saturdays and Sundays.

Palladius writes of visiting such a monastery between Alexandria and Nitria, in which some 5000 men were living, some alone, some in pairs, others in groups. Beyond that community, and yet attached to it, were 600 hermits living out their solitary lives in the Great Desert. Seven bakeries on the mountain of Nitria provided food for all these people. Indeed, all the communities were totally self-sufficient. The religious lived in separate cells rather as the hermits did in the desert, but they had their work and their prayers in common.

Each monastery traded with the outside world, beside providing services in the form of hospitals, hostels and schools. Anybody was welcome to stay in the guest-house, the only stipulation being that a healthy visitor who stayed longer than a week was expected to contribute to the community by working in the bakery, garden or farm. Any guest who was able to read could borrow a book from the monastery library.

Novices were received from all walks of life; only hardened criminals who could not be expected to adhere to any rule were excluded. However, admission was not made easy. All candidates were kept for several days outside the monastery wall until the doorkeeper had taught them prayers, psalms and the elementary duties of a monk. Then those who still wished to pursue their calling were brought into the monastery and clothed in the sleeveless linen tunic and hooded cape of a novice.

The rules of each monastery may have varied slightly, but most of them had an elaborate penitential code. In the desert monasteries the abbot gave spiritual instruction in the open air under a palm tree, and his discourses were preceeded by individual public confessions. From this custom there arose a code which the Irish Church was to adapt to its own purposes. Finnian's idea of penance was that contraries are to be cured by contraries, and that the penance for certain sins should consist in the practice of the opposite virtue. His penitential, the oldest surviving example of its kind, influenced Gildas, who recommended penances for thirty sins or offences. To give one example: 'If anyone because of drunkenness is unable to sing the psalms, being stupified and without speech, he is deprived of dinner.' Such Gilbertian arrangements were incorporated by Columbanus into his rule for his monastery in Gaul.

However the penances were ordered, the abbot was usually a soul friend to his monks and regulated the amount of asceticism that each individual should practice. In taking on this role he acted as guide and counsellor. His relationship to his monks was far removed from the fanatical attachment between guru and disciple that we sometimes witness today. The purpose of the soul friend was to lead the postulate to a state of spiritual freedom, in which he would be able to walk his own path with no external guide constantly showing him the way.

The idea of monasticism first came to the West in the second half of the fourth century, when Athanasius, Bishop of Alexandria and champion and protector of the Egyptian monks, visited Rome in 359. He had with him two disciples of Antony, Ammon and Isidore. For the Celtic Church, however, the chief monastic impulse and model did not come so much from Athanasius' mission as from the work of his slightly younger contemporary, John Cassian, who may well have been a Celt himself if the conjectures that he was born in Scythia are well founded.

Although Cassian's birthplace is uncertain, we know that he spent many years as a young man with a community in Bethlehem, and that it was from there that he went with his friend Germanus to visit the hermits of the Egyptian desert. His urge to visit them was so strong that he agreed to almost any undertaking that would enable him to do so. He promised his superiors that he would make a very rapid journey and return as soon as possible. That promise was broken, and although he felt guilty all his life at having betrayed his word, he consoled himself with the conviction that it was a lesser fault than that of losing the opportunity for spiritual development which he could gain in the desert. So he stayed in Egypt for seven years.

When Cassian eventually came into Gaul to set up his own monastery, he brought with him many of the ideas held by his teacher and close friend John Chrysostom, whose adherence to the Gnostic teachings of Origen had brought him into disrepute in Rome. Like Origen, he held to such doctrines as the pre-existence of the soul, and these beliefs were passed on to Cassian, who embodied many of them in his major writings, *The Institutions* (a treatise on monastic rule) and *The Conferences* (published in 425 and dedicated to Honoratus, whose monastery on the Riveria island of Lèrins is supposed to have been visited by Patrick). In that later work Cassian shows sympathy with the teachings of the British monk Pelagius, who had made a very favourable impression on Jerome at this time, although his doctrine questioning the existence of original sin rapidly led him to be declared anathema. Nevertheless in the thirteenth *Conference*, Cassian argued for the effectiveness of salvation through will, and although that book was long omitted from any collection of his works to receive an imprimatur, it was no doubt read in the monastery that he established near Marseilles.

In many ways Cassian is the originator of Western monasticism, for it was his rule that Benedict adopted; but for the model on which the Celtic monastic system was founded we must look farther north to central France. It was at Tours that Martin founded his settlement at Marmoutier, probably about fifty years before Cassian came to Marseilles. Ninian is said to have visited Martin's monastery and named his own White House (probably the first stone church to be built in Britain) in its honour. In any case, information about Marmoutier was widespread throughout the fifth century, by which time Sulpicius Severus' life of Martin had reached Ireland. In the fifth and sixth centuries Ninian's Candida Casa became a college as well as a monastic settlement and many new abbots and monks were trained there.

There is nothing to see of that college at Whithorn now, where a village has grown up under the Anglian translation of the Latin name Ninian gave to his monastery. Cattle graze in the field of rough grass opposite the ruins of a twelfth-century abbey, and the archaeologists have covered over the site where they discovered that the scholars once worked at their Latin texts. Among them were Enda, who was to establish a monastic school of his own on the Aran Islands in Galway Bay, and Finnian of Moville, who took part in Columba's education.

There is more to be seen at the site of the sixth-century college of Beuno at Clynnog Fawr, southwest of Carnarvon. This tiny roadside village has a vast church, which is joined by a stone passageway (reputed to date from the seventh century) to a great hall, which stands on the site where Beuno founded his school.

However, the greatest of the Welsh colleges was founded by Illtut, probably on the site of the present village of Llantwit Major between Bridgend and Cardiff. An early life of his most famous pupil, Samson, written some time before the ninth century, claims that Illtut was the most learned of all the Britons in the knowledge of both the Old and the New Testaments and in every branch of philosophy, poetry, rhetoric, grammar and arithmetic. Samson, who had been brought to Illtut as a child by his parents, proved to be so brilliant that he incurred the jealousy of his fellow students; and about the same time as the young Kentigern left Serf's monastic school at Culross because of the envy of his colleagues, Samson went west to Caldy Island, where he eventually became abbot. About 545 he started travelling again, this time going south through Cornwall to Brittany, but when he knew that he must leave Wales, he took his library with him. According to the life, he obtained a chariot from Ireland and filled it with his books.

The other great Welsh monastic college was that founded by David at Menevia to the north of St Bride's Bay. The rules of his monastery, where the monks were only allowed to drink water and had to follow a vegetarian diet, were of unusual rigidity. Gildas even complained that David urged his monks to abjure the use of oxen and place the yoke on their own shoulders. In his opinion such actions were worse than ridiculous and could lead a monk into a false position in which he would 'prefer fasting to charity, vigils to justice'. Nevertheless David's monastery attracted such outstanding Irish visitors as Finnian of Clonard, Brendan of Clonfert and Finnbar, founder of the monastery at Cork.

Although Patrick is said to have founded a monastic school at Slane in County Meath, many leaders of the Irish Church came to study in Scotland and Wales, as their druidic predecessors had done before the coming of Christianity. It was to become a two-way traffic. Both Samson and Gildas spent some months in Ireland, Cybi was four years on the Aran Islands and Cadoc studied for three years at Lismore in Waterford. On both sides of the water the monastic colleges and schools were the only source of learning. Glendalough became so renowned that Aengus, an Irish bard of the eighth century, declared it to be 'the Rome of the Western world'. Children as young as seven were sent to these monastic schools, and the teaching was done in small groups in a kindly, sensible fashion. Columba's first alphabet was impressed on a cake which he was allowed to eat when he had learned his letters.

That boy grew into the man who founded his own monastic schools at Derry, Durrow and Kells in Ireland; but his greatest foundation was on the Scottish island of Iona, where Oswald, prince of Northumbria, received his education when he was a youth in exile. That schooling influenced the course of history throughout seventh-century Northumbria, for it inspired Oswald to create a daughter foundation for Iona on the high-tide island of Lindisfarne. There Anglo-Saxon boys were trained as priests and missionaries and developed a loyal affection for the Irish Church. These students were taught Latin and were expected to write religious verses in that tongue as well as to learn the Psalms and passages of the Bible by heart. They also learned some secular subjects such as mathematics, astronomy and the art of agriculture.

After Whitby, the existence of the Celtic monastic schools in the north acted as a brake on the 'reforms' which Canterbury planned to institute. To counteract their influence, the Roman monastic schools of Wearmouth and Jarrow were founded. They were intended to replace Iona and Lindisfarne, but today it is those two places that attract visitors and pilgrims. They still keep the spirit of the Celtic Church alive and form an epilogue to this story, although they both have less to show of the original Celtic settlements than the ruined monastic sites of Ireland. The cluster of churches at Ciaran's Clonmacnoise and those founded at Glendalough by 'Kevin the Virtuous, the warrior with the fair hair', stand open to the sky, but they still bear witness to the immense amount of activity that took place there for several centuries.

The standard pattern for these monastic settlements was a walled enclosure in which the cells and oratory were contained, and where the larger churches were built in later years. By the time of the Norse invasions of Ireland a defensive round tower, such as you can still see at Glendalough, Clonmacnoise and Kells, was added to this cluster of buildings. Only one Celtic monastery, and that the simplest, remains intact. The six beehive cells and the two oratories on the rock of Skellig Michael, 8 miles off the coast of Kerry, never boasted a college. The men who lived in that community were virtual hermits who followed the Egyptian desert pattern of choosing a place of extreme isolation. Nevertheless, even in the monastic cities each monk probably lived almost as austerely, although subject to fewer hazards, than the men on the Skellig. They all built their cells with their own hands, slept on beds of skins, used stone pillows covered with bracken or dry leaves, and their only furniture consisted of a wooden bench, a cross and a rush lamp.

Some people have argued that Celtic monasticism really started through the formation of religious tribes as related groups of people turned to Christianity. Whether that is so or not, it is certain that the monastic settlements became the centres of territorial communities. They provided a haven for people of all sorts of talents and skills, and they had space both for the evangelists and the solitary contemplatives. They were places in which the outsider could find an identity, and where the gregarious could find a true social purpose.

It was a movement in which women had an important part to play. At Tabennesi there was a community of 400 women, who lived on the opposite side of the river from the monks, and who were visited by a priest and deacon on Sundays. In some ways that formed a model for the double monasteries of the Celtic Church, although in those institutions the abbess was always the superior. It has been argued that her status originated in Christ's words to Mary and John: 'Woman, behold thy son, son behold they mother.' The *Catholic Encyclopaedia*, which declares that 'maternity is a form of authority derived from nature, while that which is paternal is merely legal', offers another explanation for the superior status of the abbess.

We can never know if such thoughts were in Patrick's mind when he gave the veil to Monnine, an older contemporary of Brigid, who established a community of fifty nuns near Newry. Brigid's own work at Kildare was matched a hundred years later by the royal-born Hilda, who entered the religious life at the age of thirty-five, and who reformed the abbey of Whitby eight years later, modelling it on the rule of the Irish Church. Here she built up libraries and provided an education in Latin and literature for clerics such as Bossa, who became Bishop of York in 678. But her most famous pupil will always be the abbey's cowherd Caedmon, who composed the first Anglo-Saxon verses on biblical themes from the Creation to Christ's Passion and the Last Judgement.

One of Hilda's contemporaries was Ebbe, daughter of Ethelfrith, king of Northumbria, who became a nun at Coldingham to the north of Berwick and was later made abbess there. If reports are to be believed, this well-born patron of Wilfrid was less interested in religion than in fine living. Adomnan of Iona had reason to reproach her for allowing her nuns to spend their time in weaving fine clothes and adorning themselves like brides, while both the monks and nuns of this double monastery neglected prayers and vigils. Ebbe's niece and pupil Etheldreda left Coldingham in 673 to found her own double monastery as Ely, where she is said to have lived a life of austerity and penance. Her own life may have been blameless, but her foundation, which provided a rich living for her sister and nieces, was probably as wealthy and luxurious as Coldingham itself.

With Ebbe the slide away from the early monastic ideals had begun. Wilfrid was such a favourite of hers

that when Ecgfrid's queen, Ermenburga, was suddenly
taken ill on a visit to Coldingham in 681, Ebbe
interpreted the sickness as divine punishment for a slight
to the prelate. The rot that started in Ebbe's abbey
culminated in the behaviour of many wealthy and
tryranizing abbots who eventually drew the tragedy and
vandalism of the Dissolution on themselves. They had
moved far from the piety of such men as Cedd, bishop of
the East Saxons, who was educated at Lindisfarne and
was obviously imbued with much of the humility of his
teacher Aidan, who refused to ride a horse on his
journeys lest it separate him from the common people. In
658, when Cedd was given land for the foundation of a
monastery at Lastingham in North Yorkshire by Oswin's
son, Oethelwald, he fasted for forty days on the moor
before consecrating the land on which he was to build. In
doing so he was following a traditional custom which
marked the foundation of each Welsh *llan*.

At that time it was the practice to dedicate a monastic
oratory to the founder of the settlement or to the saint
whose disciples were establishing a daughter house. It
was not long after the Synod of Whitby, which
inaugurated a rush of dedications to Peter, that apostolic
dedications became common. They replaced the earlier
ones to such an extent that Northumbria soon had no
dedications left for its beloved Aidan. Dedications to the
Virgin Mary came much later; in fact, they did not
appear in Ireland until the twelfth century.

In the early years of the Celtic Church the founding
saint might establish a simple tribal settlement as
members of large family groups became converted to
Christianity. Eventually some of these settlements grew
into the great monastic schools, while others dwindled
into remote hermitages. In either case a spring or well
would mark the place where the settlement was begun,
and it was these wells which were to become venerated
as the goal of pilgrimages. They remained so long after

Henry VIII had dispersed the great wealth of the abbey churches.

Even in the sixth century the accumulation of monastic lands had become a problem. Although Gildas conceded that abbots were not to be condemned for possessing cattle and vehicles, he found it necessary to advise that monasteries should not seek to add to their possessions unduly. Of course, many of them did. Yet it is clear that there were always small communities content to settle on land that was sufficient to supply them with their needs, and to divide and colonize new and uninhabited waterside areas when their numbers became too large.

These water sources, with their reputed healing properties, offer the key to Celtic monasticism. They provided the means whereby groups of people were enabled to settle and to embark on their own spiritual journeys, unrestricted by the dogmas and hierarchies of large political institutions. It is significant that one of Rome's chief complaints against the organization of the Celtic Church was that the abbot of any monastery, however small, held more authority than the bishops.

10

Holy Springs and Wells

Because life is impossible without a constant supply of fresh water, the source has always been held sacred. Every settlement has to be situated near a well or a spring, and the provisions for guarding the water have always been clearly defined. One of the ways of preserving a well is to give it a name, an identity. When Isaac pitched his tent in the valley of Gerar and re-dug the wells originally sunk by his father Abraham, he called them by their original names (Genesis, 24, 18); and when his servant had to contend with the native herdsmen for new wells, they established their rights over the water sources by naming the places: Esek, Sitnah, Rehoboth and Shebah.

There is a close connection between naming and dedication, and it was the same desire to protect the water supply that made the pagan Celts call their wells after the local and tribal deities and to dedicate many of them to the great goddess Anu. The Celtic tribes who settled in the fertile valley of the Boyne regarded the river as miraculous. They believed that it had no terrestrial source, but flowed from the other world out of the well of Segais, which nourished the nine hazel trees of wisdom. Such a belief sanctified and preserved the actual waters of the Boyne.

Many holy wells which are to be found near the site of

ancient churches were also clearly used by prehistoric and pagan settlements and revered as holy long before they were sanctified by a Christian saint. Such a well is the one near Capel Finnan on the shores of Luce Bay in Galloway. There the sparse ruins of the rectangular Celtic church stand close to a group of cairns, stone circles, monoliths and cup-and-ring-marked stones all indicative of a flourishing community, even pre-Celtic in origin.

Much later, as new settlements were formed and as the families by the old water supplies became Christian, the pagan dedications were often transferred to the saint with whom the place was associated, and later still to Anne, mother of the Virgin, whose name might well be derived from that of Anu, and which in any case can easily be confused with it. In the case of those wells which carry a dedication to a Celtic saint, we can believe that as the waters supported the holy men, so they by their sanctified lives blessed the waters; and so the pagan well worship was transformed to Christian ends. Often the wells and well pools, like the one fed by the underground river which flows beneath the north transept of St Patrick's Cathedral in Dublin, were used for baptisms.

Despite such practices, the early Church was always uneasy about the veneration that people instinctively gave to wells. Dedicating them to the saints only consolidated the instinct for water worship which was at one time ingrained into human consciousness. That reverence is something we have sadly lost with the advent of easy supplies of piped water, and our casual attitude can have disastrous consequences. That was not the case in the so-called Dark Ages. In its early struggles against the multifarious pagan deities of place, described by Gildas as 'the diabolical idols of my country, which almost surpassed in number those of Egypt', the continental Church, at both the Synod of Arles in 452 and the Council of Tours in 567, found itself forced to denounce the practice of well worship in a way that suggests it was almost impossible to stamp it out. So it proved to be, for in ninth-century England the Saxon King Egbert had to prescribe a three-year penance for anyone who was discovered to be keeping a vigil by a well rather than in 'God's church'.

The Church was wiser when it turned the natural human instinct to revere the water source to its own purpose, and followed Gregory's edict that objects of pagan worship should be dedicated to Christ. So water was made sacrosanct by calling wells and springs by the names of the saints, and even by allowing the practice of well dressing, the annual glorification of a well, to continue as a Christian practice. This custom is still going on today, most notably in Derbyshire, where many of the wells which spring out of the limestone are annually adorned with pictures of biblical scenes produced by pressing quantities of flower petals into frames of clay.

The church even managed to make its own use of the Celtic cult of the severed head, which always became particularly potent when a skull could be associated with water. Like many primitive people, the Celtic Iron Age warriors believed that the spirit, which gave a person his powers of virtue and energy, resided in his head and was still there after death. So warriors became headhunters, and in that way they felt they could acquire all the strength and courage of a vanquished enemy. If the skull of such a head were to be put in a well or spring, then it was believed that the waters would have great potency and be able to restore anyone who drank there. Even greater healing could be obtained if a person were to drink directly from the skull, and prophetic power could actually be acquired in that way.

The link between the cult of the severed head and the potency of well water was preserved in the hagiographies of the saints, and so effectively that the

Ox of St. Luke with halo and cross. Gospel of St. Matthew. Book of Kells.

mysterious beheadings of holy men quickly found a place in local folklore. In many of these stories the well is supposed to have sprung out of the ground on which the saint's head lay before it was miraculously reunited with the body. The most famous of these stories concerns Wynefride, whose holy well in Clwyd is still a place of devotion, healing and pilgrimage. She was a niece of Beuno, and it was her refusal to marry which led to her decapitation by her infuriated suitor. A fountain sprang out of the rock onto which her severed head fell. Her uncle joined it back to her body and so restored her to life and to a career as abbess of the nunnery which grew up beside the waters.

The story of the Welsh saint Decuman is another example of the combined cult of the severed head and the sanctity of water. When the saint crossed the Severn Sea and landed on the north Somerset coast, he was killed by an assassin, who no doubt feared that the foreigner would take over both his territory and his water supply. Decuman was standing in prayer when he was attacked and decapitated. To the astonishment of his adversaries he bent down to pick up his head, carried it a little way downhill to the well whose waters still spring out today, and washed it carefully before setting it back on his body. In that way he established his right over the well for ever. A similar feat was performed by Nectan a little farther along the coast. He carried his severed head to a well half a mile away from the place where he was beheaded.

Through these stories, the church could establish that those who came to seek healing at a well did so through the power of Christ's saints. In those cases in which a well was also regarded as an oracle – for a severed head, as in the medieval story of *Gawain and the Green Knight*, had the power of prophetic speech – the message could be regarded as having a divine origin. Both healing and prophecy thus came through the spirit of a man or woman who had been a notable servant of the one God.

In time, as always happens, the serious aspect of prophecy became lost in superstitious fortune-telling. Many a well, like the one dedicated to Cybi at Llangybi, was used to forecast the outcome of affairs of the heart. A girl who wanted to know if her lover's protestations were honest and serious had only to spread her pocket handkerchief on the surface of the water. If the water pushed the handkerchief south everything would be all right, but if it floated north then she knew that she had been deceived. More ghoulish was the ritual that took place at the well of the Holy Rood in Bodmin each Holy Thursday. There the children dropped rush crosses into the well to find out if they would still be alive the following year. A cross that sank presaged doom.

Despite all the supernatural wonders, the greatest miracle a well can perform is to produce water, especially in times of drought. Throughout the country people will still talk of wells that retained a constant supply of water in even the driest summers. This beneficence was thought to be due to the power of the tutelary deity or the sanctity of the saint to whom the well was dedicated. On the other side of the coin, as we read in the Book of Job, wicked and faithless friends can be compared to wells that vanish in hot weather; and it was often believed, in pagan and early Christian Britain, that evil powers could dry up a well or pollute its waters if the god or saint who protected it was not properly placated.

In a sense we have seen this happen in our own day, when through careless and greedy uses of technology we have poisoned a water supply. In the wet spring of 1986, even before the disaster at Chernobyl, cattle, chicken and dogs in the Bonny Bridge area of Stirlingshire started to sicken and die in alarming numbers, until one farmer though to end the disaster by taking his stock off tap water, which was presumably fouled by industrial processes. The need to preserve the purity of the water supply is one of the first essentials for any community, and it is possibly for that reason that the sanctity of wells has been preserved throughout the centuries. People step warily at sacred places, and cattle, which can so easily spread disease, are not allowed to use them as water holes.

It is sad to see how often the wells, so carefully protected when they provided a village with its main source of water, have been allowed to fall into decay now that the water comes from the mains. Sometimes, despite neglect, the buildings which once protected the well remain, as they do at the spring which Beuno sanctified by his settlement at Clynnog Fawr. This little rectangular enclosure is open to the sky. It has a stone seat running along the inner sides, and the place could still be made into a tiny sanctuary. But, alas, the well itself has become almost clogged up by the amount of rubbish that has been allowed to accummulate in its spring-fed basin.

On the other hand, at some places people have still taken great care of the wells, surrounding them with carefully tended gardens. I think particularly of the terraced garden which leads up to Glastonbury's Chalice Well; of the flowers planted round the well where David's mother, Non, had her chapel at the northern head of St Bride's Bay; and of the cultivation which is going on around the long-neglected well of Aldhelm at Doulting in Somerset.

In all those places the sanctity of the wells is preserved and we are reminded again that the worst attack any group of people can inflict on another is to desecrate the water supply. When the power of sanctity is not sufficient to preserve a well, then people might try to save themselves by endowing the spring with maleficent powers which can bring disaster to anyone who tampers with the waters. I believe that this is the reason why some springs and wells are reputed to give power to those who would use them for evil purposes and for putting a curse on their enemies. Elian's well at Llandrillo yn Rhos was sometimes used to that evil end, the cursing being made the more efficacious by the aid of some of the more violent passages of the Old Testament. The chosen scripture had to be read by the owner of the well, who then gave the applicant some of the water to drink. The man who wished to make the curse then drank a little and threw the remainder back into the well, describing the retribution which he hoped would overtake his enemy as he did so. This ritual was repeated three times.

It is far more common, however, for the miraculous powers associated with wells to be benevolent and concerned with healing. Celtic tales, such as the Irish myth of the battle of Moytura, tell of dead warriors being restored for further fighting after they were flung into wells; and the druid Merlin was said to have been cured of his madness by the power of the waters of a well in the forest of Brocéliande to the south of St Malo. Similar miracles of healing are associated with the saints' wells of Christian times. Often the miracles which resulted from the use of these waters were specific for different parts of the body. The most common cures that took place at wells were concerned with diseases of the eyes. This may have come about through an almost homeopathic sensitivity, for the spring or well was often thought of as the eye of the landscape. On the other hand, those who looked into a forbidden or secret well could expect to be blinded, a superstition which would be encouraged by anybody wanting to preserve their own well or to make an unreasonable charge for the use of the water.

Less easily explicable are the reputations that some wells had for the cure of toothache, epilepsy or madness, when the waters were used in a way that could channel the powers of the saint to whom they were dedicated. In the case of mental disorders the rituals involved were frequently reminiscent of the cruel shock treatment of the snake pit. At Fillan's well near Tyndrum the wretched patient was immersed in the waters of the pool fed by the spring and then forced to spend the following night tied to a wooden frame in the priory church on the mountainside, with his head in the stone font and the saint's handbell placed on his body. If he was sane enough to struggle so that the ropes which bound him were found to be slackened by the following morning, then it was believed that a cure had been effected.

The most popular wells were those which were said to confer fertility on those who drank from them or who bathed in their waters. Many of these wells were particularly dedicated to Brigid in her role as midwife, wetnurse and guardian of women in labour. Their potency prevails to this day, and throughout Ireland you can find Brigid wells, like the one outside Lahinch by the cliffs of Moher, which bear evidence in the form of tokens, ikons and rosaries that women still come here to ask the saint's blessing on their marriages and on the children they hope to bear.

A scarlet fuschia hangs over the grotto that forms an entrance to the Lahinch well, which is at the bottom of a hillside garden, stepped and paved. Among the rosaries and the holy pictures that are left there you will find instructions to the pilgrims, telling them how they should walk around the two levels of the garden before making any invocation to Brigid at the spring. The garden is spacious enough for a whole village of maidens to hold a vigil in, and indeed they did so every autumn, before setting off for the fairs and the horse races at which men were wont to choose their wives, while there was a pause in the farming year.

The holy tokens left at the Brigid wells are altogether more elaborate than the coins and pins which were often thrown into water, and the rags which one can still see tied to trees and bushes surrounding springs and wells. This practice has partly degenerated into the throwing of coins into wishing wells. It seems almost instinctive to throw money into water in the hopes that it will cause a wish to be granted or that it will be returned tenfold. This inexplicable urge has possibly grown out of a feeling that something must be offered to a well. Where pins take the place of coins, it can only be that the magic of metal is in some way associated with the powers of the water. Sometimes the bent pins are thought to represent the disease that the well has cured, and in that cause they share a symbolism with the rags which are tied to nearby trees.

Another explanation for the rags is that they hold the votaries' prayers in a sacred place long after those who made them have gone away. At the end of the last century the folklorist John Rhys was told that in North Wales it was felt to be essential that the rags so used should be composed of pure wool in its natural state which would contrast with the wrought metal of the pins and coins.

Until a few years ago, at Madron in the moors to the north of Penzance, the rags used to be tied to a small tree growing in the compound of the ruined baptistry, whose waters came from the nearby holy well. They are not there now; instead you will find them on the bushes beside the duckboard path that leads to the pool where the well originates. The water here is flanked by ferns and rough, flat stones, and in summer the little glade is alive with birds and butterflies attracted from the surrounding woodlands.

The fact that the rags have been moved out of the more obviously sacred enclosure, in which services are still sometimes held, may be significant. But it is also important that although you can now walk almost dryshod to the pool, for years people had to wade to get to it. The destruction of that holy well and its conversion into a waterhole for cattle can be attributed to Sir Henry Shrubsall, governor of Pendennis Castle during the Commonwealth. He was anxious to discourage the pilgrims who came to visit the waters on account of their reputed healing powers. That reputation had gained strength from the story of John Trelille. He was a twenty-eight-year-old cripple who had been forced to walk on his hands since he was twelve because of the contraction of the sinews of his legs. In 1641 he was cured after three visits to Madron's Well.

Although Trelille's cure was recorded as authentic by Joseph Hall, Bishop of Exeter, the enthusiasm it engendered was frowned on by the extreme Puritans. However, pilgrims are never easily discouraged, and wells will always be sought out for their potential for physical and spiritual healing. Many wells are marked by the pilgrims who have visited them. A Maltese cross with wide-spreading arms in a form common to the Celtic Church was carved centuries ago on a flat stone by the side of the lane that leads to a well sacred to the saintly Issui in the Black Mountains. This half-hidden well probably drew pilgrims to its waters long before folk tradition claimed that a holy man called Issui made his hermitage in the dingle, but after that its power increased.

The waters were soon found to be an effective cure for all manner of diseases. In the eleventh century a wealthy traveller from the continent was cleansed of his leprosy by them, and in gratitude he left a hatful of gold in order that the church which stands there today could be built at the top of the hill. Possibly the unknown benefactor actually laid his money in one of the niches in the enclosure which still surrounds the spring. These, which once held sacred images and relics of the saint, are now often filled with flowers by walkers, who still find the place holy.

For people are still drawn to wells with the

compunction that we all have to seek the Grail, however that may be interpreted. For the Christian chalice has much in common with the pagan cornucopia, and both are contrived from the human need to try to form an image that will contain the whole source of physical and spiritual life. Indeed, the best known of the British holy wells, the Chalice Well in Glastonbury, makes this quite explicit. Whether or not Joseph of Arimathea brought the cup that was used at the Last Supper to Somerset, as the medieval monks of the wealthy abbey claimed he did, this spring, which gave water to the first settlers here, still has the power to attract thousands of pilgrims each year. If the story of its connection with the Grail could be categorically disproved, they would still make the journey. For this well has come to symbolize a need that could never be met by any actual cup, and whose fulfillment is different for every individual.

11

Pilgrims and Pilgrimages

The desire to go on pilgrimage, to seek for some spiritual or material benefit to be found away from home, is a deep human instinct, common to people of all religions and creeds. It stems partly from the belief that a person's strength abides in the place where his god is, and a quick reflection on the cult of local tribal deities makes it easy to see how such a belief can be translated into geographic terms. When the Israelites under King Ahab had soundly beaten the forces led by the Syrian King Benhadad, the counsellors of the vanquished army gave this advice to their leader: 'Their gods are gods of the hills; therefore they were stronger than we; but let us fight against them in the plain, and surely we will be stronger than they' (I Kings, 20, 23).

From instances such as that it has been argued that the habit of pilgrimage arose out of tribal displacement. People who had left the bare hillsides of their homelands for the more fertile valleys found themselves needing to return from time to time to the mountains of their tribal gods. It is an instinct that persists in the urge to trace our family histories, and has arisen with the incessant mobility brought about by the industrial revolution. It has become an obsession among many people today, taking a physical form as they abandon the genealogies and the county record offices and actually journey to their place of origin. Fittingly enough, the most common location for such latter-day pilgrimages is Ireland, thronged each summer by Americans moved to trace their roots.

It is an instinct fortified by the senses of sight and touch. Pilgrims will always be prepared to undergo physical hardship in order to see the holy places and touch the revered objects. This led to the importance of the cult of relics which was to become such a source of greedy dispute in the Middle Ages. Yet honest pilgrimages have continued. They were no new thing when they became incorproated into the life of the Celtic Church, and it is unlikely that they will ever cease in some form or other. This instinct for pilgrimage is distinct from the urge to wander which I described in chapter 7, although like it in many ways. The main difference is that the pilgrim always has a specific goal and purpose in mind, and usually expects to return to his home base, whereas the true wanderer looks for no settled abode.

When primitive man felt that his strength and energy lay with his native gods, it was natural that he should return to the place where they were located in order to draw on their spiritual and physical power for his own use. In the same way the adherents of the early Church felt that their faith could be deepened and their physical ills remedied by prayers and meditations performed at a site associated with a particularly holy person, or with Christ himself. There was also a feeling that any vow that was made in a holy place had a particularly solemn and binding strength, as though the local deity or saint who was associated with that spot was acting as a witness to the words that were spoken. For this reason many pilgrimages marked the beginning of new undertakings and often heralded an entrance to the monastic life.

By the third century Christians were going on pilgrimage to the Holy Land, and it was not long before they were joined by men and women from Roman Britain. After Jerome's disciple Paula, a widow of Rome, had travelled with her daughter Eustochium to Jerusalem and Egypt, she urged her fellow citizen, the widow Marcella, to join her in Israel. 'Whosoever is noblest in Gaul comes hither,' she wrote, 'and Britain though divided from us yet hastens from her land of sunset to these shrines known only to her through the scriptures.' Possibly some of these British pilgrims stayed at the hospice on the Mount of Olives run by Melania, a friend of the Church historian Rufinus and a follower of the teachings of Origen. If they did they would have found her ideas sympathetic to the emerging philosophy of the Celtic Church.

In the seventh century, Columba's successor, Adomnan wrote out the account of a pilgrimage to Jerusalem, Bethlehem, Alexandria and Constantinople ('without any doubt the capital of the Roman Empire') as it was verbally described to him by the Gallic bishop Arculf. It was a laborious undertaking, both in the journeying and the reporting. Like a good journalist, the abbot of Iona took down the verbatim story on tablets and then wrote it out 'on parchment in the form of a short essay' which fortunately is still extant. The fact that Adomnan further declared that he undertook all this labour at a time 'when the work of caring for the church kept me under pressure of business and overwork poured in from every direction all day long' emphasizes the value that he put on recording pilgrimages to the holy places.

By this time pilgrims were already seeking out the holy sites of these islands. Bardsey, Ninian's Whithorn, David's Menovia as well as Iona itself all had the power to attract hordes of pilgrims. Of these places only Iona, with its daughter island Lindisfarne, still draws large numbers of people. They go there in their thousands, and more and more people are making a true pilgrimage, travelling great distances on foot to reach the goal. For in the matter of pilgrimage the journey, which is a form of preparation for the arrival, is all-important.

That is one of the reasons why involved rituals were designed for those who sought healing at the holy wells; and why, nowadays, the sick who are taken to Lourdes or to our own Holywell in Clwyd make proper preparations for their visits although they are usually unable to walk there. It was always so. There is little difference in spirit between the medieval provision for carrying the sick in litters to the holy places and our own method of taking the chronically ill across Europe to Lourdes in the voluntarily subscribed 'Jumbulances'. Those who remain at home and are taken to Holywell find the pool of Wynefride surrounded by an imposing superstructure of medieval buildings. In those almost stagnant waters (do they ever ripple like those of Bethseda, I wonder?) men and women (at segregated hours) can dip themselves and stand on the very spot where the saint was beheaded.

The holy places are not only a source of healing. They used also to be considered a fount of wise counsel. As the Greeks went to Delphi to consult the oracle, so right through the Middle Ages the Scottish kings came to Ninian's shrine at Whithorn to give thanks for their victories against the English and to seek advice on their future campaigns. Whithorn was considered to be a particularly powerful place and pilgrims came there in such throngs each year that in 1441 Margaret, Countess of Douglas, felt herself justified in claiming an indulgence in recompense for her expense in making repairs to the road bridge crossing the river Bladnoch, just to the north of Ninian's shrine.

Such crowds of people naturally brought prosperity to the places they visited, and there is no doubt that this affected the veneration of the relics in the possession of Celtic monasteries and abbeys. They were to become valued as much for the immediate and tangible material benefits that they brought as they were for their spiritual significance. Inevitably a certain amount of not-so-honest trading in saints' bones went on as avidly in the Celtic Church as it did in the Church of Rome. It had to. By the time of the second Nicene Council in 787 bishops were being threatened with deprivation if they consecrated a church which lacked some holy relic.

Because of the trade in relics, and indeed the occasional thefts that this decree engendered, many Church leaders came to regard the act of pilgrimage with a wary suspicion if not outright hostility. In their different ways both Columba and Bede warned people of the hypocrisy of making long and expensive journeys to seek a spiritual good which they could find as well amid the tedium of the dull routines of home. However, we know that Columba himself was a great traveller, and that although Bede probably never ventured out of northeast England, he did go on at least one pilgrimage in that area, visiting the Yorkshire abbey of Lastingham founded by Cedd. He had a personal reason for doing so, for Trumhere, one of the monks who had been trained by Cedd's brother Chad, was Bede's tutor, and it was from him that he developed his love and respect for the humble and compassionate bishop.

Pilgrimages made out of such genuine respect were indeed honourable; so were those that were made as a form of penance, for travelling was at best uncomfortable and frequently dangerous. Many people were swept out into the Irish Sea as they attempted to cross the dangerous currents surrounding Bardsey Island, and the hazards on land, from wild beasts, bandits and difficult terrain, were almost as great. The strenuous effort involved in making long journeys across the Continent was too much for many people. Indeed, we hear of pilgrims who expected, even hoped, to die when they reached their goal, as Bede (Book v.7) says Caedwalla, king of the West Saxons, did. He abdicated his throne in 688 so that he might journey to Rome in order to be baptized there, hoping 'to die shortly after his baptism, and pass from this world to everlasting happiness.' His desire was granted; and his example of pilgrimage was followed by his successor, Ina, who handed over his throne after he had reigned for thirty-seven years and set out for Rome 'wishing to spend some of the time of his earthly pilgrimage in the vicinity of the holy places.'

Bede assures us that many English people followed Ina's example. 'Both noble and simple, layfolk and clergy, men and women alike.' Among them was Guthlac's sister Pega, who was to die in Rome. According to a not uncommon custom, her heart was brought back to her native fens and became an object of pilgrimage in its turn. It still lies in a stone reliquary in Peakirk parish church. Every year from 833 Wiglaff, king of Mercia, went to Guthlac's shrine at Croyland, and no doubt he then went on the oratory which housed Pega's heart.

At home, in places where no obvious dangers presented themselves, penitential journeys were made throughout the Middle Ages by pilgrims who walked barefoot to Our Lady's shrine at Walsingham or climbed the tor overshadowing Glastonbury Abbey with dried peas in their socks. The penitential aspects of pilgrimage were embodied in the tenth-century laws of the Anglo-Saxon king Edgar. They declared: 'It is a deep penitence that a layman put down his weapons and travel far barefoot and nowhere pass a second night and fast and watch much and pray fervently, by day and by night, and willingly undergo fatigue, and be so squalid that iron come not on hair or nail.'

Ritual forms of penitential discomfort were taken to an extreme in Ireland, where rituals of long fasting and nightly vigils were devised for those seeking pardon at mountain chapels and island shrines. Until quite recently pilgrims might arrive fairly comfortably by train from Dublin to seek Patrick's Purgatory on Lough Derg, but once they had crossed the water their shoes were removed, and they had to exist on a diet of milkless, sugarless tea and dry bread as they made their observances at the shrine and kept at least one night's vigil.

Some pilgrimages achieved the status of an athletic obstacle race. Penitents who dared the dangerous sea crossing to Skellig Michael could expiate their sins by climbing a precipitous rock stack (the Needle's Eye) and then traversing a rocky promontory ('the stones of pain') jutting into the sea, before scrambling up a further height (the Eagle's Nest), and so on to a narrow ledge to kiss the cross cut into the rock there. Such physical feats are somewhat reminiscent of the hordes of dancing, flagellating pilgrims who writhed their way across Europe in the Middle Ages; a craze started at the instigation of Rainier, a thirteenth-century hermit of Perugia, and also of the cavalcades of crusaders jousting with death on their military pilgrimages.

Yet despite these man-made miseries, the progress in search of absolution and forgiveness could be a strangely joyful matter, and it is still so reflected in the pageantry of the Breton *pardonnes*. The joy comes out of the companionship. Pilgrimage with all its hazards and discomforts was rarely a solitary matter. We do not simply have to take Chaucer's word for the merry company that many people found on their journeys. It is still being re-enacted today. The Dutchman Kosti Simmons, who leads back-packing pilgrims as far afield as Campostella in northern Spain, as well as on more modest walks to the holy places of Britain, has noticed how the companionship of the journey puts doctrinal differences into a proper perspective. When the goal is reached, the solemnity of the place must demand the grace of silence; but the journey always seems to have been an occasion for discourse of all sorts. People's minds are generally more active when they are walking, and pilgrims have probably always been ready to talk among themselves about both religious and secular matters. If there was no one to talk to they might read as they journeyed. The early lives of Ninian recount that he did so even as he walked across the Alpine passes on his way to Rome.

The need to walk with a social purpose, as well as for the health of one's soul, finds a secular fulfilment in today's sponsored walks, which contain many of the elements of pilgrimage. It is significant that this apparently pointless way of raising huge sums of money has been so universally adopted. On the face of it, it would seem to be more reasonable for the walking (undertaken for pleasure and exercise) to exist in its own right divorced from any cause, but that is not so. Two elements are present in the sponsored walk which are absent from direct donations. One is the obvious publicity given to the cause by the public walk undertaken on its behalf; the other is more complex and hidden. By paying another person to undertake a walk for a valuable cause, the donor is re-enacting the part of those rich men who paid their servants to undertake a penitential pilgrimage on their behalf. It is an arrangement which leaves everybody feeling good.

The package holiday is one step further removed from the original notion of pilgrimage, and yet there will always be those who treat the sacred journey as a jaunt. Chaucer's folk, who longed to go on pilgrimage as soon as April had broken the frosts of winter, were taking a well-earned holiday once the spring lambs were established and before the hard work of the growing season had begun. The hermits of the Egyptian desert were well aware that, among the pilgrims who came to seek their wisdom, there were those whose travelled mainly for the adventure of the journey and whose strongest motive was pure curiosity. Yet those hermits of ancient Egypt, and the ones who live on Athos today, formed a living goal for pilgrimage. Their words of wisdom could be as much sought after as the divine oracles of the sacred shrines and wells, and we have already seen that one reason why a hermit would chose to settle in an inaccessible place was to make it difficult, if not dangerous, for anyone who came to seek him out. That way his words would be the more fully valued.

The whole stress of pilgrimage centres on the outward journey. We hear very little of the return. After all the stories have been told, Chaucer's pilgrims are entertained at the end of their journey by a sermon on the seven deadly sins, delivered by the Parson. We know nothing of how they amused themselves thereafter. If Chaucer ever intended to produce a second group of tales for the return journey, it was an unfulfilled project. Yet questions remain. Having made the great journey of a lifetime, and in most cases that is what it would be, how did a pilgrim of the seventh or eighth century face the hazards of the no less dangerous return? Was he upheld by the benefits he had received, or saddened that even after so much effort no miraculous cure had taken place, no new spiritual insight had been granted? It could be so, yet I do not think that many disillusioned people made the return journey, judging by my experience of those sick people who today return from Lourdes and Walsingham apparently no better than when they set out. Healing is not necessarily the same thing as a cure, and although it sounds superficially like a rather lame excuse, it is usually the case that those who return are better equipped psychologically to cope with their disabilities.

In any case there is always the satisfaction of a journey accomplished. We cannot know if the pilgrims of the Celtic Church came back from the shrines they visited with the sort of tokens that were given as souvenirs to the pilgrims of the Middle Ages, but it is most probable that they did. It is possible too that although the Celtic pilgrimages took place long before the passing of the vagrancy laws, which demanded that pilgrims should be identified, there was even then some sort of badge to signify the status of these travellers. This in itself would be a source of pride and a mark of achievement on the return.

Even in those early times traders were, no doubt, making a living out of selling tawdry trinkets which would become mementos of a memorable experience, and which would also enable the pilgrims, like the Palmer in *Piers Plowman*, to show proof that they had been to many shrines and 'walked full widely in wet and dry'. More pertinently, the tokens or 'blessings' with which the pilgrims returned home served as reminders of the strengths they had gained at the holy places. They fulfilled the same function as the 'two mules' burdens of earth' which Naaman asked the prophet Elisha to grant him so that he might always be reminded of the vow he made when his leprosy was washed away (II Kings, 5, 17).

Whatever they carried with them, the pilgrims on their outward and their return journeys made a public profession of their religious faith as well as undertaking a personal quest. For pilgrimage has always partly served as public demonstration, and not always of a religious nature. This was made clear as J. J. Jusserand reminds us in his *English Wayfaring Life in the Fourteenth Century*. To go on a pilgrimage to the place where one of the king's enemies had been murdered was to register a protest against the government. It is most probable that during the seventh century many pilgrims to the sites sacred to the earlier saints of the Celtic Church were registering their disapproval of Wilfrid and the decision that had been made at Whitby.

Of one thing we can be sure. At that stage the act of pilgrimage had not run into the sort of licentious disrepute which was to cause it to be condemned by

Langland and Wycliffe. The people who visited the sites
of the early Church were still motivated by the druidic
spirit which held that some places on the earth's surface
were particularly sacred to the gods, and they approached them with a reverence for the earth itself
which later pilgrims were hardly aware of.

So what are we doing, those of us who belong to no
particular Church, when we find ourselves compelled to
seek out the holy places, the sites of the ancient
monasteries of Glendalough and Iona, the local holy
wells and the hermits' caves, or to follow the crosses
which mark the ancient pilgrim routes across hills and
moors? Are we merely indulging a historical fascination,
or does the journey have any special significance for our
own lives? What are we looking for in the vanished
world of the Celtic Church?

I believe that at a time when so many of our public
pilgrimages are made in the form of demonstrations to
the locations of death (the missile sites and the nuclear
power stations), these other pilgrimages affirm a life
lived close to the realities of nature and in defiance of
military bureaucracy, in whatever institution that
inhuman, impersonal power is vested. Certainly there is
no surer way of linking the centuries together, and of
feeling a part of the whole long body of the human race,
than by making one of the journeys across landscape that
has been familiar to generations of pilgrims. And
alongside the general public urge to pilgrimage goes the
search of the individual soul, the initiation journey,
which is as much an internal as an external matter. By
the fourteenth century the act of pilgrimage was being
explicitly equated with the soul's search in Guillaume de
Degouilleville's *Le Pèlerinage de la Vie Humaine*. I am
certain that it was being so considered long before his
time.

Epilogue

Twenty years after the fateful decision at Whitby, the people of these islands endured a terrible physical clash between adherents of differing Christian beliefs. It set the model for those that have besmirched our history ever since. In 684 Ecgfrid, king of a Northumbria which was almost totally subservient to Canterbury, took it upon himself to promote his beliefs (and increase his power and wealth) by invading northern Ireland, where people still remained loyal to the Celtic Church. The monks who compiled *The Anglo-Saxon Chronicle* were deeply distressed by this event. Beside the entry for the year they wrote: 'Ecgfrid sent an army against the Scots [i.e. the northern Irish] and Berht his earldorman was with it, and miserably they afflicted and burnt God's church.'

The memory of that outrage did not die. In the twelfth century William of Malmesbury recorded the event in his history of Britain and wrote of Ecgfrid's reign that the king 'overwhelmed the Irish with widespread slaughter, a harmless race of men, who with native innocence never attempted to do anyone a mischief.' William of Malmesbury was probably drawing on Bede, the monk of Jarrow, who was a lad of eleven when the outrage took place, and who later wrote how his king had 'brutally harassed those inoffensive people [the Irish] who had always been so friendly to the English, and in his hatred he spared neither churches nor monasteries. The islanders resisted force by force as well as they could, and implored the merciful aid of God, praying Heaven long and earnestly to avenge them.' In a sense their prayer was answered. The following year, acting against the advice of Cuthbert, who did all he could to restrain the violent monarch, Ecgfrid decided to swing his attack against the Picts who upheld the Celtic Church in northeast Scotland. This time his victims were too fierce for him, and on 20 May he was killed at the battle of Nectansmere. Sadly the disputes and the pattern of bloodshed that he started lived on. They are still with us today.

The tragedy of inter-Christian killings in the seventh century was followed by the violence of the attacks on this country by the pagan, philistine and pirate Danes during the next 200 years. Right thorugh the eighth century the marauding Viking fleets plundered the coastal monasteries and abbeys. In 793 they sacked Lindisfarne, causing so much havoc that the monks fled, taking with them the uncorrupted body of Cuthbert, the relics of Aidan and the glorious manuscript that we know as the Lindisfarne Gospels. Two years later the vandals attacked the island of Iona, slaughtering the monks on the white sands of the northeastern corner of the island on a beach which is still known as the Bay of Martyrs.

In parts of northeastern Scotland and all over Ireland, from Kells and Glendalough in the east to Clonmacnoise in the west, tall round towers were built to provide lookout places and refuge. Their entrances are always a good 6 feet above the ground. Yet it was the east coast of England from Coldingham in Northumbria to Reculver in Kent that was the most vulnerable. Finally, in 865, the Danish raiders came in such a force that the whole of eastern England was overcome. The remnants of Christianity survived in the west and found its champion in Alfred.

The wretchedness caused by the Danish invasions is recorded over and over again in the entries of *The Anglo-Saxon Chronicle* and in the latter local histories compiled by various abbeys. In the twelfth century a chronicler in Peterborough, looking back 300 years, wrote these impassioned words: 'For then came the Danes, servants of the Devil, and like mad dogs and robbers issuing of a sudden from their dens, even so they land of a sudden from their ships and come on a people that suspected no ill, burning cities, villas and monasteries and slaughtering old men, young men and children.'

Now in Peterborough Cathedral, a few miles from Guthlac's Croyland, you can see a stone memorial, carved soon after the event, in tribute to the monks who were killed in such a raid in 897. In a nearby chapel the arm of King Oswin was kept as a holy relic until the eleventh century. He was a seventh-century king of Deira, one of the two parts into which Northumbria was then divided, and was revered as saint and martyr after he lost his life in a battle with Cadwalla, the pagan king of Mercia. Now the chapel, to which pilgrims once came to seek a blessing from that holy relic, is reserved for prayers for peace.

Indeed, it it those who seek peace on earth before any other good who have the greatest affinity with the Celtic Church today. They may well look back across fifteen centuries for the inspiration that will provide a hope for our own desperate times. Some peace movements, such as Pax Christi, are based formly on an institutional church while going beyond rigid denominations and boundaries. Others spring out of the so-called New Age (a term that I find as misleading as the misnomer of the Dark Ages) and flow with the free workings of a spirit that cannot be even loosely tied to any establishment. These two attitudes are closer to each other than many people appreciate, and both of them can be understood in the light of what we know of the Celtic Church.

The liturgy for a peace vigil which some members of

Pax Christi have devised in support of the Greenham women follows the Jewish and Celtic division of measuring time by night and day. So it runs the course of the Sabbath, from 6 o'clock on Friday for twenty-four hours. The time between is divided up by appropriate readings from the Psalms in a way that the Celtic saints would certainly have understood; and during the course of the twenty-four hours the stages of Christ's passion and resurrection, and the hope that these bring for the redemption of the world, are offered for meditation.

It is fitting in more than the most obvious way that women should have taken the leading part in organizing this vigil, although, of course, men are welcome to join in. Like the current debates on the ordination of women, it revives the spirit of the double monasteries of the Celtic Church, ironically exemplified by Whitby, whose abbess was never happy with the dispensations of Canterbury, and who kept her foundation Celtic in spirit although complying with the Roman form. Because of her gentle persistence, Archbishop Theodore found it wiser to allow the Celtic double monasteries to continue, and Hilda's gentle and effective example still inspires many women today in their efforts to construct a more justly balanced society.

Such a society is envisaged by the newly formed Eirene Community, which arose from the rubble of the peace chapel inside the fence at Molesworth which was destroyed by the Minister of Defence two weeks after the Easter of 1986. This group, like many others, is based on the idea of spiritual and positive peace making, and its aim is to create and demonstrate peace by helping people to act out of quiet reflection. Other Christian groups, such as Jonathan Robinson's Grail Trust in Somerset and the Othona Community in Dorset, offer space and time to people of any faith or none so that they can find their own inner peace and live from it.

The people who run such groups may be likened to the

Irish Culdees (a name which comes from *Ceil de*, 'the servant of God') who carried on many of the traditions of the Celtic Church. The Culdees gave their lives entirely to God, although, unlike monks, they were still allowed to retain some private property. They based themselves on the rule of Maelruain, an eighth-century abbot of Tallaght near Dublin, which he compiled with the help and inspiration of Angus, a hermit widely renowned for his piety.

For several hundred years a group of Culdees lived in the monastery on the island of Loch Leven in south-eastern Scotland. Indeed, there were thirteen Culdee settlements in that country in the early Middle Ages. The record for the one on Iona dates from 1164, and in that century the monk Giraldus Cambrensis wrote of a Culdee house on Bardsey Island. Although the stricter members of the sect remained celibate, there are records of married men being attached as Culdees to the monastery of the Irish Clonmacnoise in the eleventh century. The canons of St Peter's in York were known as Culdees until the term fell into general disuse in the thirteenth century.

The spirit of the Culdees is certainly alive in the community now based on Columba's Iona. The members of this group spend at least two weeks of each year on the island, and devote the rest of their time to working for peace among the distress and turbulence of our inner cities. For it is the cities that have become the wastelands, while the rural areas have lost the dangerous isolation and privation that were to be found there until the beginning of this century.

The work done by the members of the Iona community is comparable to that of the worker priests who submerge themselves in the industrial lives of the people; and it brings reflections on the political implications of liberation theology. The French writer Jean Daniélou has likened the dedication of such people, who leave the comfort of ordered religious institutions for the monotonous deprivation of the industrial conveyor belts, to the sacrifice of the early hermits, who deliberately cut themselves off from a reasonably comfortable and companionable life. 'My factory,' he wrote, 'is my desert.'

Daniélou was writing before the flood of unemployment, which is all too slowly forcing us to change our whole attitude to an industrial consumer society. Many people are trying to find the new answer by setting up small community groups which aim at a life style that will enable them to approach a state of self-sufficiency. In this way they are unwittingly beginning to reconstruct the early Celtic monasteries in which groups of like-minded people lived in almost a tribal manner. This has been going on long enough now for the founders of such communities to imbue a place with a spirit which persists after their physical death, in the same way that the Welsh *llans* and the Irish monastic settlements retained the influence of their founders for many centuries.

At the time that those early Christian communities were forming Britain was witnessing the collapse of an ordered world that had seemed immutable. The ruins of the Roman walls, villas and garrisons, such as those which Cuthbert was taken to see in Carlisle, reminded the people of a vanished order which was no less secure for being oppressive. Liberation from the Roman Empire did not bring the paradise on earth that many had hoped for. Famine and pestilence still raged, and land-hungry hordes from across the water could not be stopped from invading the islands. The adherents of the Celtic Church found that their strength lay in each other, and in their belief in the eternal love of Christ which offered the ultimate hope for the world.

Fifteen hundred years later we find ourselves in much the same position as our ancestors were after the collapse of Imperial Rome; and this may account for the revival of

S. Chadde

An old drawing of St. Chad from a MS in the Bodleian Library
(Reproduced by permission of the Bodleian Library)

interest in our Celtic inheritance. It is marked by the archaeological explorations at present going on at Whithorn, which are revealing more about the daily lives of the people who were attached to the monastic institutions and colleges; and also by the increased membership of the Orthodox Church in this country. That above all revives the almost lost link with the Christianity of our early saints. For the Orthodox throughout the world have always revered Ninian, while his fellow countrymen have come near to neglecting him.

Yet whether we are formally Christian or not, we need the example of Ninian's life, and that of Columba and the other Celtic saints whom he inspired, if we are to survive our present predicament. For liberated from the oppressive mores and institutional organizations of our forefathers, we find ourselves adrift in a world where science, which for so long promised us ever-increasing comforts and conveniences, is now in the position of the sorcerer's apprentice, unable to control its own power to destroy on an unimaginable scale.

When so many people are looking towards the East to find an answer to this catastrophe and a peace that the Western churches seem unable to provide, it is important to recall that we have in our own lands a tradition that can well be an inspiration towards a way of life that promises peaceful companionship in this world, and one which shows us the way in which time can be transcended.

Many people in the established institutions find the doctrines and practices of the Celtic Church (particularly the legacy of the Irish penances) both crabbed and quirky. In the same way many of the rituals of the Buddhist monasteries can strike Western people as raucous and incomprehensible: for neither Celts nor Buddhists are geared into our tight timescales and the logical systems of technology. That does not mean that they cannot show us a way out of the confusion that human intellect divorced from feeling has led us into.

The past is not necessarily another country. The best of it can be made to live again here. I believe that what the Celtic Church has to teach us about tolerance, persistence and a tough but gentle kindliness offers a real hope for our troubled world. Perhaps our only hope.

Bibliography

A.M. Allchin (ed.), *Solitude and Communion: Papers on the Hermit Life*, SLG Press, Oxford, 1977.

Peter F. Anson, *The Call of the Desert: the Solitary Life in the Christian Church*, SPCK, 1966.

Geoffrey Ashe, *Land to the West: St Brendan's Voyage to America*, Collins, 1962.

Peter Bamm, *Early Sites of Christianity*, Faber, 1957.

Bhagavad Gita, translated and introduced by Juan Mascaré, Penguin Books, 1962.

H.A. Blair, *The Kaleidoscope of Truth: Types and Archetypes in Clement of Alexandria*, Churchman Publishing Ltd, Worthing, 1968.

P. Hunter Blair, *Roman Britain and Early England*, Sphere, 1963.

P. Hunter Blair, *The World of Bede*, Secker & Warburg, 1970.

J.W. Willis Bond, *The Celtic Church of Wales*, D. Nutt, 1897.

Janet and Colin Bord, *Sacred Waters: Holy Wells and Water Lore in Britain and Ireland*, Granada, 1985.

B.C. Boulter, *The Pilgrim Shrines of England*, Philip Allan, 1928.

A.C. Bouquet, *Hinduism*, Hutchinson University Library 1962.

E.G. Bowen, *Saints, Seaways and Settlements in the Celtic Lands*, University of Wales Press, 1969; revised 1977.

William Bright, *Chapters of Early English Church History*, Clarendon Press, 1887.

Raymond E. Brown, *The Community of the Beloved Disciple*, Geoffrey Chapman, 1979.

Sir Ernest A. Wallis Budge, *The Wit and Wisdom of the Christian Fathers of Egypt, translated from the Syrian Version*, Oxford University Press, 1934.

Dom Cuthbert Butler, *Benedictine Monachism*, Longman Green, 1924.

Henry Chadwick, *The Early Church*, Methuen, 1914; Penguin Books, 1967.

Nora K. Chadwick, *Age of the saints in the Early Christian Church*, Oxford University Press, (2nd edition) 1963.

Nora K. Chadwick, *The Celts*, Penguin Books, 1970.

Nora K. Chadwick, *Early Brittany*, University of Wales Press, 1969.

Owen, Chadwick, *John Cassian*, Cambridge University Press, 1st edn, 1950; 2nd edn, 1968.

Rotha Mary Clay, *Hermits and Anchorites of England*, Methuen, 1914.

Peter Crossley-Holland, Non-Western Music: the Jews, *Pelican History of Music*, vol. I, Penguin Books, 1960.

Jean Daniélou, *The Theology of Jewish Christianity*, Darton, Longman & Todd, 1964.

Jean Daniélou, *The Dead Sea Scrolls and Primitive Christianity*, translated by Salvator Attanasio, Helicon Press, Maryland, 1955.

Jean Daniélou, *Primitive Christian Symbols*, Compass Books, Burns Oates, 1961.

Jean Daniélou, *The Lord of History*, Longman Green, 1958.

Daniel-Rops (ed.), *The Miracle of Ireland*, Burns Oates, 1959.

Gregory Dix (trans.), *Hippolytus' Apostolic Tradition*, SPCK, 1937.

Gilbert H. Doble, *St Illtud*, University of Wales Press, Cardiff, 1944.

Christopher Donaldson, *Martin of Tours: Parish Priest,*

Mystic and Exorcist, Routledge & Kegan Paul, 1980.

Evagrius Ponticus, *The Praktikos: Chapters on Prayer*, translated and edited by John Endes Bamberger, Cistercian Publication, Spencer, Mass., 1970.

George Ewart Evans, *Horse Power and Magic*, Faber, 1979.

Harvey, Falk, *Jesus the Pharisee: a New Look at the Jewishness of Jesus*, Paulist Press, New York, 1985.

Felix, *Life of Guthlac*, edited, with translation by Bertram Colgrave, Cambridge University Press, 1956.

Paul Gallico, *The Steadfast Man: a Life of St Patrick*, Michael Joseph, 1958.

Erwin R. Goodenough, *An Introduction to Philo Judaeus*, Blackwell, 1962.

Louis Gougaud, *Christianity in Celtic Lands*, Sheed & Ward, 1932.

Hugh Graham, *The Early Irish Monastic Schools*, Talbot Press, 1923.

Robert Graves, *The White Goddess*, Faber, 1961 edn.

D.J. Hall, *English Medieval Pilgrimage*, Routledge & Kegan Paul, 1965.

Sydney Heath, *Pilgrim Life in the Middle Ages*, T. Fisher Unwin, 1911.

Michael Herity and George Gogan, *Ireland in Prehistory*, Routledge & Kegan Paul, 1977.

Christina Hole, *English Shrines and Sanctuaries*, Batsford, 1954.

R.C. Hope, *Legendary Lore of the Holy Wells of England*, Elliot Stock, 1983.

Spiro Kostof, *Caves of God*, MIT Press, 1972.

Casimir Kucharek, *The Byzantine-Slav Liturgy of St John Chrysostom*, Alleluia Press, Canada, 1971.

Jacques Lacarrière, *The God-Possessed*, translated by Roy Markham, Allen & Unwin, 1963.

Lloyd Laing, *Late Celtic Britain and Ireland 400–1200*, Methuen, 1975.

John Lanigan, *Ecclesistical History of Ireland*, Simpkin & Marshall, London, 1829.

J.A. Lyons, *The Cosmic Christ in Origen and Teilhard de*

Chardin, Oxford University Press, 1982.

John Campbell MacNaught, *The Celtic Church and the See of Peter*, Oxford University Press, 1927.

John L. Gough Meissner, *The Celtic Church in England after the Synod of Whitby*, Martin Hopkinson, London, 1929.

Eleanor C. Merry, *The Flaming Door*, Floris, 1983.

J.H. Middleton, *Illuminated Manuscripts in Classical and Mediaeval Times*, CUP, 1892.

J.T. Milik, *The Book of Enoch*, Oxford University Press, 1976.

J.R. Morris, 'The Dates of the Celtic Saints', *Journal of Theological Studies*, vol. 17, 1966.

H.V. Morton, *Through Lands of the Bible*, Methuen, 1938.

Daphne Pochin Mould, *The Celtic Saints Our Heritage*, Clonmore & Reynolds, Dublin; Burns Oates & Washbourne, 1956.

Jacob Newsner, *Midrash in Context*, Fortress Press, Philadelphia, 1983.

Jacob Newsner, *Judaism in the Beginning of Christianity*, SPCK, 1984.

Carl Nordenfalk, *Celtic and Anglo-Saxon Painting*, Chatto & Windus, 1977.

Christian O'Brien, *The Megalithic Odyssey*, Turnstone, 1983.

Peter O'Dwyer, *Spiritual Reform in Ireland 750–900*, Editions Tailliura Dublin, 1981.

Joan O'Grady, *Heresy*, Element Books, 1985.

John O'Hanlon, *Lives of the Irish Saints*, Burns Oates, 1875.

Elaine Pagels, *The Gnostic Gospels*, Weidenfeld & Nicolson, 1979.

Palladius: The Lausiac History, edited and translated by Robert T. Meyer, Longman Green, 1965.

Susan M. Pearce, *The Kingdom of Dumnonia*, Studies in the History and Tradition in South-Western Britain, AD 350–1150, Lodenek Press, Cornwall, 1978.

Eric Peterson, *The Angels and the Liturgy*, translated by Ronald Walls, Darton, Longman & Todd, 1964.

John Rhys, *Celtic Folklore*, 2 vols., Oxford University Press, 1901.

Alwyn and Brinley Rees, *Celtic Heritage*, Thames & Hudson, 1961.

D. Talbot Rice, *The Beginnings of Christian Art*, Hodder & Stoughton, 1957.

Alec Robertson, 'Plainsong', *Pelican History of Music*, vol. I, Penguin Books, 1960.

J. Armitage Robinson, *Barnabas, Hermas and the Didache*, SPCK, 1920.

T.W. Rolleston, *Myths and Legends of the Celtic Race*, Harrap, 1911.

Norman Russell (trans.), *The Lives of the Desert Fathers*, Mowbray, 1980.

John Ryan, *Irish Monasticism*, Talbot Press, Dublin, 1931.

R.V. Sellers, *The Council of Chalcedon*, SPCK, 1953.

John Sharkey, *Celtic Mysteries*, Thames & Hudson, 1975.

Alfred P. Smyth, *Warlords and Holy Men: Scotland AD 80–1000*, Edward Arnold, 1984.

Jonathan Sumption, *Pilgrimage*, Faber, 1975.

Charles Thomas, *The Early Christian Archaeology of North Britain*, Oxford University Press, 1971.

E.A. Thompson, *Saint Germanus of Auxerre and the End of Roman Britain*, Boydell Press, 1984.

Nikolai Tolstoy, *The Quest for Merlin*, Hamish Hamilton, 1985.

E.W.F. Tomlin, *In Search of St Piran*, Lodenek Press, Padstow, 1982.

Joseph Wilson Trigg, *Origen: the Bible and Philosophy in the 3rd Century Church*, John Knox Press, Atlanta, 1949.

Helen Waddell, *Beasts and Saints*, Constable, 1934.

Helen Waddell, *The Desert Fathers*, Constable, 1936.

A.W. Wade-Evans, *Welsh Christian Origins*, Alden Press, Oxford, 1934.

J. Charles Wall, *Shrines of British Saints*, Methuen, 1905.

J.W.C. Wand, *The History of the Early Church to 500 AD*, Methuen, 1937.

Sister Benedicta Ward, *The Wisdom of the Desert Fathers*, SLG Press, Oxford, 1975.

Kurt Weitzman, *Late Antique and Early Christian Book Illustration*, Chatto & Windus, 1977.

James Wilkie, *Saint Bride*, T. N. Foulis, 1913.

Reginald Maxwell Woolley, *Coptic Offices*, SPCK, 1930.

Appendix

Bede: Book v. Chapter 21., which sets out in full the different methods of calculating the date of Easter; and the discrepancies over the tonsure. The letter to the Pictish king was written about 710.

Abbot Ceolfrid sent the king of the Picts architects to build a church, and with them an epistle concerning the Catholic Easter and Tonsure.

At that time Nechtau[1], king of the Picts, inhabiting the northern parts of Britain, taught by frequent meditation on the ecclesiastical writings, renounced the error which he and his nation had till then been under, in relation to the observance of Easter, and submitted, together with his people, to celebrate the Catholic time of our Lord's resurrection. For performing this with the more ease and greater authority, he sought assistance from the English, whom he knew to have long since formed their religion after the example of the holy Roman Apostolic Church. Accordingly he sent messengers to the venerable Ceolfrid, abbot of the monastery of the blessed apostles, Peter and Paul, which stands at the mouth of the river Wire[2], and near the river Tyne, at the place called Gyrthum[3], which he gloriously governed after Benedict, of whom we have before spoken; desiring, that he would

1. Nechtan
2. Wear is the name of the river now
3. Jarrow

write him a letter containing arguments, by the help of which he might the better confute those that presumed to keep Easter out of the due time; as also concerning the form and manner of tonsure for distinguishing the clergy; not to mention that he himself possessed much information in these particulars. He also prayed to have architects sent him to build a church in his nation after the Roman manner, promising to dedicate the same in honour of St. Peter, the prince of the apostles, and that he and all his people would always follow the custom of the holy Roman Apostolic Church, as far as their remoteness from the Roman language and nation would allow. The reverend Abbot Ceolfrid complying with his desires and request, sent the architects he desired, and the following letter:

'To the most excellent lord, and most glorious King Nechtau[1], Abbot Ceolfrid greeting in the Lord. We most readily and willingly endeavour, according to your desire, to explain to you the catholic observance of holy Easter, according to what we have learned of the Apostolic See, as you, devout king, with a religious intention, have requested; for we know, that whenever the Church applies itself to learn, to teach, and to assert the truth, which are the affairs of our Lord, the same is given to it from heaven. For a certain worldly writer most truly said, that the world would be most happy if either kings were philosophers, or philosophers were kings. For if a worldly man could judge truly of the philosophy of this world, and form a correct choice concerning the state of this world, how much more is it to be wished, and most earnestly to be prayed for by the citizens of the heavenly country, who are travelling through this world, that the more powerful any persons are in this world, the more they may labour to be acquainted with the commands of Him who is the Supreme Judge, and by their example and authority may

1. Nechtan

induce those that are committed to their charge, as well as themselves, to keep the same. There are three rules in the Sacred Writings, on account of which it is not lawful for any human authority to change the time of keeping Easter, which has been prescribed to us; two whereof are divinely established in the law of Moses; the third is added in the Gospel by means of the passion and resurrection of our Lord. For the law enjoined, that the Passover should be kept in the first month of the year, and the third week of that month, that is, from the fifteenth day to the one-and-twentieth. It is added, by apostolic institution, in the Gospel, that we are to wait for our Lord's day in that third week, and to keep the beginning of the Paschal time on the same. Which threefold rule whosoever shall rightly observe, will never err in fixing the Paschal feast. But if you desire to be more plainly and fully informed in all these particulars, it is written in Exodus, where the people of Israel, being about to be delivered out of Egypt, are commanded to keep the first Passover, that the Lord said to Moses and Aaron, "This month shall be unto you the beginning of months; it shall be the first month of the year to you. Speak ye unto all the congregation of Israel, saying, In the tenth day of this month, they shall take to them every man a lamb, according to the house of their fathers, a lamb for an house." And a little lower, "And ye shall keep it until the fourteenth day of the same month; and the whole assembly of the congregation of Israel shall kill it in the evening." By which words it most plainly appears, that thus in the Paschal observance mention is made of the fourteenth day, not that the Passover is commanded to be kept on that day; but the lamb is commanded to be killed on the evening of the fourteenth day: that is, on the fifteenth day of the moon, which is the beginning of the third week, when the moon appears in the sky. And because it was on the night of the fifteenth moon, when by the slaughter of the Egyptians,

Israel was redeemed from a long captivity, therefore it is said, "Seven days shall ye eat unleavened bread." By which words all the third week of the same month is decreed to be kept solemn. But lest we should think that those same seven days were to be reckoned from the fourteenth to the twentieth, God immediately adds, "Even the first day ye shall put away leaven out of your houses; for whosoever eateth leavened bread, from the first day until the seventh day, that soul shall be cut off from Israel;" and so on, till he says, "For in this self-same day I will bring your army out of the land of Egypt.' Thus he calls that the first day of unleavened bread in which he was to bring their army out of Egypt. But it is evident, that they were not brought out of Egypt on the fourteenth day, in the evening whereof the lamb was killed, and which is properly called the Passover or Phase, but on the fifteenth day, as is most plainly written in the book of Numbers. "Departing therefore from Ramesse on the fifteenth day of the first month, the next day the Israelites kept the Passover with an high hand." Thus the seven days of unleavened bread, on the first whereof the people of God were brought out of Egypt, are to be reckoned from the beginning of the third week, as has been said, that is, from the fourteenth day of the first month, till the one-and-twentieth of the same month, that day included. But the fourteenth day is noted down separately from this number by the name of the Passover, as is plainly made out by what follows in Exodus; where when it is said, "For in this same day I will bring your army out of the land of Egypt;" it is presently added, "You shall keep it a feast by an ordinance for ever. In the first month, on the fourteenth day of the month at even, ye shall eat unleavened bread, until the one-and-twentieth day of the month at even. Seven days shall there be no leaven found in your houses." Now, who is there that does not perceive, that there are not only seven days, but rather eight from the fourteenth to the one-and-twentieth, if the fourteenth be also reckoned in the number? But if, as by diligent study of Scripture appears to be the truth, we reckon from the evening of the fourteenth day to the evening of the one-and-twentieth, we shall certainly find, that the same fourteenth day gives its evening for the beginning of the Paschal feast; so that the sacred solemnity contains no more than only seven nights and as many days. By which our definition is proved to be true, wherein we said, that the Paschal time is to be celebrated in the first month of the year, and the third week of the same. For it is really the third week, because it begins on the evening of the fourteenth day, and ends on the evening of the one-and-twentieth. But since Christ our Paschal lamb is slain, and has made the Lord's day, which among the ancients was called the first after the Sabbath, a solemn day to us for the joy of his resurrection, the apostolic tradition has so inserted it into the Paschal festivals as to decree, that nothing in the least be anticipated, or detracted from the time of the legal Passover; but rather ordains, that the same first month should be waited for, pursuant to the precept of the law, and accordingly the fourteenth day of the same, and the evening thereof. And when this day should happen to fall on the Sabbath, every one in his family should take a lamb, and kill it in the evening, that is, that all the churches throughout the world, composing one catholic church, should provide bread and wine for the mystery of the flesh and blood of the unspotted Lamb "that took away the sins of the world;" and after the solemnity of reading the lessons and prayers of the Paschal ceremonies, they should offer up these things to the Lord, in hopes of future redemption. For that same night in which the people of Israel were delivered out of Egypt by the blood of the lamb, is the very same in which all the people of God were, by Christ's resurrection, delivered from eternal death. Then, on the morning of the Lord's day, they should celebrate the first day of the

Paschal festival; for that is the day on which our Lord, with much joy of pious revelation, made known the glory of his resurrection. The same is the first day on unleavened bread, concerning which it is distinctly written in Leviticus, "In the fourteenth day of the first month, at even, is the Lord's Passover. And on the fifteenth day of the same month, is the feast of unleavened bread unto the Lord; seven days ye must eat unleavened bread; the first day shall be most solemn and holy." If therefore it could be that the Lord's day should always happen on the fifteenth day of the first month, that is, on the fifteenth moon, we might always celebrate Easter at the very same time with the ancient people of God, though the nature of the mystery be different, as we do it with one and the same faith. But in regard that the day of the week does not keep pace exactly with the moon, the apostolical tradition, which was preached at Rome, by St. Peter, and confirmed at Alexandria, by Mark the Evangelist, his interpreter, appointed that when the first month was come, and in it the evening of the fourteenth day, we should also wait for the Lord's day, which falls between the fifteenth and the one-and-twentieth day of the same month. For on whichever of those days it shall fall, Easter will be properly kept on the same; as it is one of those seven days on which the unleavened bread is ordered to be kept. Thus it comes to pass that our Easter never deviates from the third week of the first month, but either observes the whole, or at least some of the seven legal days of unleavened bread. For though it takes in but one of them, that is, the seventh, which the Scripture so highly commends, saying, "But the seventh day shall be more solemn and holy, ye shall do no servile work therein," none can lay it to our charge, that we do not rightly keep our Lord's Paschal day, which we received from the Gospel, in the third week of the first month, as the law prescribes. The catholic reason of this observance being thus explained;

the unreasonable error, on the other hand, of those who, without any necessity, presume either to anticipate, or to go beyond the term prescribed in the law, is manifest. For they that think the Lord's day of Easter is to be observed from the fourteenth day of the first month till the twentieth moon, anticipate the time prescribed in the law, without any necessary reason; for when they begin to celebrate the vigil of the holy night from the evening of the thirteenth day, it is plain that they make that day the beginning of their Easter, whereof they find no mention in the law; and when they refuse to celebrate our Lord's Easter on the one-and-twentieth day of the month, they wholly exclude that day from their solemnity, which the law often recommends as memorable for the greater festival; and thus, perverting the proper order, they place Easter day in the second week, and sometimes keep it entirely in the same, and never bring it to the seventh day of the third week. And again, because they rather think that Easter is to be kept on the sixteenth day of the said month, and so to the two-and-twentieth, they no less erroneously, though the contrary way, deviate from the right way of truth, and as it were avoiding to be shipwrecked on Scylla, they run on and are drowned in the whirlpool of Charybdis. For when they teach that Easter is to be begun at the rising of the sixteenth moon of the first month, that is, from the evening of the fifteenth day, it is manifest that they altogether exclude from their solemnity the fourteenth day of the same month, which the law firstly and chiefly recommends; so that they scarcely touch upon the evening of the fifteenth day, on which the people of God were delivered from the Egyptian servitude, and on which our Lord, by his blood, rescued the world from the darkness of sin, and on which being also buried, he gave us hopes of a blessed repose after death. And the same persons, taking upon themselves the penalty of their error, when they place the Lord's day of Easter on the twenty-second day of the month, openly transgress and exceed the legal term of Easter, as beginning the Easter on the evening of that day in which the law appointed it to be finished and completed; and appoint that to be the first day of Easter, whereof no mention is any where found in the law, viz. the first of the fourth week. And they are sometimes mistaken, not only in defining and computing the moon's age, but also in finding the first month; but this controversy is longer than can or ought to be contained in this letter. I will only say thus much, that by the vernal equinox, it may always be found without the chance of an error, which is the first month of the year, according to the lunar calculation, and which the last. But the equinox, according to the opinion of all the Eastern nations, and particularly of the Egyptians, who exceed all other learned men in that calculation, usually happens on the twelfth day of the kalends of April, as we also prove by horological inspection. Whatever moon therefore is at the full before the equinox, being on the fourteenth or fifteenth day, the same belongs to the last month of the foregoing year, and consequently is not proper for the celebration of Easter; but that moon which is full after the equinox, or on the very equinox, belongs to the first month, and in it, without a doubt, the ancients were wont to celebrate the Passover, and we also ought to keep Easter when the Sunday comes. And that this must be so, there is this cogent reason, because it is written in Genesis, that "God made two lights; a greater light to rule the day, and a lesser light to rule the night." Or, as another edition has it, "A greater light to begin the day, and a lesser to begin the night." The sun, therefore, proceeding from the midst of the east, fixed the vernal equinox by his rising, and afterwards the moon, when the sun set in the evening, followed full from the midst of the east; thus every year the same first month of the moon must be observed in the like order, so that the full moon must be either on the very day of the equinox, as was done from the beginning, or after it is gone by. But if the full of the moon shall happen to be but one day before the time of the equinox, the aforesaid reason proves that such moon is not to be assigned to the first month of the new year, but rather to the last of the preceding, and that it is therefore not proper for the celebration of the Paschal festival. Now if it will please you likewise to hear the mystical reason in this matter, we are commanded to keep Easter in the first month of the year, which is also called the month of the new fruit, because we are to celebrate the mysteries of our Lord's resurrection and our deliverance, with our minds renewed to the love of heavenly things. We are commanded to keep it in the third week of the same month, because Christ, who had been promised before the law, and under the law, came with grace, in the third age of the world, to be slain as our Passover; and rising from the dead the third day after the offering of his passion, he wished this to be called the Lord's day, and the festival of his resurrection to be yearly celebrated on the same. For we also, in this manner, only can truly celebrate his solemnity, if we take care with him to keep the Passover, that is, the passage out of this world to the Father, by faith, hope and charity. We are commanded to observe the full moon of the Paschal month after the vernal equinox, to the end, that the sun may first make the day longer than the night, and then the moon may afford the world her full orb of light; inasmuch as first "the sun of righteousness, in whose wings is salvation," that is, our Lord Jesus, by the triumph of his resurrection, dispelled all the darkness of death, and so ascending into heaven, filled his Church, which is often signified by the name of the moon, with the light of inward grace, by sending down upon her his Spirit. Which plan of salvation the prophet had in his mind, when he said, "The sun was exalted and the moon stood in her order." He, therefore, who shall contend that the full Paschal moon can happen before the equinox, deviates from the doctrine of the Holy Scriptures, in the celebration of the greatest mysteries, and agrees with those who confide that they may be saved without the grace of Christ forerunning them; and who presume to teach that they might have attained to perfect righteousness, though the true light had never vanquished the darkness of the world, by dying and rising again. Thus, after the equinoctial rising of the sun, and after the subsequent full moon of the first month, that is, after the end of the fourteenth day of the same month, all which, according to the law, ought to be observed, we still, by the instruction of the Gospel, wait in the third week for the Lord's day; and thus, at length, we celebrate our due Easter solemnity, to show that we do not, with the ancients, honour the shaking off of the Egyptian yoke; but that, with devout faith and affection, we worship the redemption of the whole world; which having been prefigured in the deliverance of God's ancient people, was completed in Christ's resurrection, to make it appear that we rejoice in the sure and certain hope of the day of our own resurrection, which we believe will happen on the same Lord's day. Now this calculation of Easter, which we show you is to be followed, is contained in a circle or revolution of nineteen years, which began long since, that is, in the very times of the apostles, especially at Rome and in Egypt, as has been said above. But by the industry of Eusebius, who took his surname from the blessed martyr Pamphilus, it was reduced to a plainer system; insomuch that what till then used to be sent about to all the several churches by the patriarch of Alexandria, might, from that time forward, be most easily known by all men, the course of the fourteenth day of the moon being regularly ordered. This Paschal calculation, Theophilus, patriarch of Alexandria, composed for the Emperor Theodosius, for a hundred years to come. Cyril also, his successor, comprised a series of ninety-five years in five revolutions of nineteen years. After whom, Dionysius Exiguus added as many more, in the same manner, reaching down to our own time. The expiration of these is now drawing near, but there is so great a number of calculators, that even in our churches throughout Britain, there are many who, having learned the ancient rules of the Egyptians, can with great ease carry on those revolutions of the Paschal times for any distant number of years, even to five hundred and thirty-two years, if they will; after the expiration of which, all that belongs to the question of the sun and moon, of month and week, returns in the same order as before. We therefore forbear to send you those revolutions of the times to come, because you only desired to be instructed respecting the Paschal time, and declared you had enough of those catholic tables concerning Easter; but having said so much briefly and succinctly, as you required concerning Easter, I also exhort you to take care to promote the tonsure, as ecclesiastical and agreeable to the Christian faith, for concerning that also you desired me to write to you; and we know indeed that the apostles were not all shorn after the same manner, nor does the Catholic Church, though it agrees in the same Divine faith, hope and charity, agree in the same form of tonsure throughout the world: in fine, to look back to remote times, that is, the times of the patriarchs, Job, the example of patience, when, on the approach of tribulation, he shaved his head, made it appear that he had used, in time of prosperity, to let his hair grow; and Joseph, the great practiser and teacher of chastity, humility, piety, and other virtues, is found to have been shorn when delivered from servitude; by which it appears, that during the time of servitude, he was in the prison without cutting his hair. Now you may observe how each of these men of God differed in the manner of their appearance abroad, though their inward consciences were alike influenced by the grace of virtue.

But if we may be allowed to speak our thoughts, the difference of tonsure is not hurtful to those whose faith is pure towards God, and their charity sincere towards their neighbour, especially since we do not read that there ever was any controversy among the Catholic fathers about the difference of tonsure, as there has been about the difference in keeping Easter, or in matters of faith. However, among all the tonsures that are to be found in the Church, or among mankind at large, I think none more worthy of being followed than that which that disciple had on his head, to whom, on his confession, our Lord said, "Thou art Peter, and upon this rock I will build my Church, and the gates of hell shall not prevail against it, and to thee I will give the keys of the kingdom of heaven." Nor do I think any more worthy to be abhorred and detested, by all the faithful, than that which that man used, to whom Peter, when he would have brought the grace of the Holy Ghost, said, "Thy money be with thee to perdition, because you thought the gift of God to be purchased for money; there is no part or lot for you in this speech". Nor do we shave ourselves in the form of a crown only because Peter was so shorn; but because Peter was so shorn in memory of the passion of our Lord; therefore we also, who desire to be saved by the same passion, do with him bear the sign of the same passion on the top of our head, which is the highest part of our body. For as all the Church, because it was made a church by the death of Him that gave it life, is wont to bear the sign of his holy cross on the forehead, to the end, that it may, by the constant protection of his sign, be defended from the assaults of evil spirits, and by the frequent admonition of the same be instructed, in like manner, to crucify its flesh with its vices and concupiscences; so also it behoves those, who have either taken the vows of monks, or have any degree among the clergy, to curb themselves the more strictly by continence. Every one of them is likewise to bear on his head, by means of the tonsure, the form of the crown which Christ in his passion bore of thorns, in order that Christ may bear the thorns and briars of our sins; that is, that he may remove and take them from us; and also that they may at once show that they, willingly, and with a ready mind, endure scoffs and reproaches for his sake; to make it appear, that they always expect "the crown of eternal life, which God has promised to those that love him," and that for the gaining thereof they despise both the adversities and the prosperities of this world. But as for the tonsure which Simon Magus is said to have used, what Christian will not immediately detest and cast it off together with his magic? Upon the top of the forehead, it does seem indeed to resemble a crown; but when you come to the neck, you will find the crown you thought you had seen so perfect cut short; so that you may be satisfied such a distinction properly belongs not to Christians but to Simoniacs, such as were indeed in this life thought worthy of a perpetual crown of glory by erring men; but in that life which is to follow this, are not only deprived of all hopes of a crown, but are moreover condemned to eternal punishment. But do not think that I have said thus much, as judging those who use this tonsure, are to be damned, in case they favour the catholic unity in faith and actions; on the contrary, I confidently declare, that many of them have been holy and worthy of God. Of which number is Adomnau, the abbot and renowed priest of Columb, who, when sent ambassador by his nation to King Aldfrid, came to see our monastery, and discovering wonderful wisdom, humility, and religion in his words and behaviour, among other things, I said to him in discourse, "I beseech you, holy brother, who think you are advancing to the crown of life, which knows no period, why do you, contrary to the habit of your faith, wear on your head a crown that is terminated, or bounded? And if you aim at the society of St. Peter, why do you imitate the tonsure of him whom

St. Peter anathematized; and why do you not rather even now show that you imitate to your utmost the habit of him with whom you desire to live happy for ever." He answered, "Be assured, my dear brother, that though I have Simon's tonsure, according to the custom of my country, yet I utterly detest and abhor the Simoniacal wickedness; and I desire, as far as my littleness is capable of doing it, to follow the footsteps of the most blessed prince of the apostles." I replied, "I verily believe it is as you say; but let it appear by showing outwardly such things as you know to be his, that you in your hearts embrace whatever is from Peter the Apostle. For I believe your wisdom does easily judge, that it is much more proper to estrange your countenance, already dedicated to God, from resemblance to him whom in your heart you abhor, and of whose hideous face you would shun the sight; and, on the other hand, that it becomes you to imitate the outward resemblance of him, whom you seek to have for your advocate with God, as you desire to follow his actions and instructions." This I then said to Adomnau, who indeed showed how much he had improved upon seeing the statutes of our churches, when, returning into Scotland, he afterwards by his preaching brought great numbers of that nation over to the catholic observance of the Paschal time; though he was not yet able to gain the consent of the monks that lived in the island of Iona, over whom he presided. He would also have been mindful to amend the tonsure, if his authority had extended so far. I also admonish your wisdom, O king, that you endeavour to make the nation, over which the King of kings, and Lord of lords, has placed you, observe in all points those things which appertain to the unity of the Catholic and Apostolic Church; for thus it will come to pass, that after your temporal kingdom has passed away, the blessed prince of the apostles will lay open to you and yours the entrance into the heavenly kingdom, where you will rest for ever with the elect. The grace of the eternal King preserve thee in safety, long reigning, for the peace of us all, my most beloved son in Christ.'

This letter having been read in the presence of King Nechtau[1], and many more of the most learned men, and carefully interpreted into his own language by those who could understand it, he is said to have much rejoiced at the exhortation; insomuch that, rising from among his great men that sat about him, he knelt on the ground, giving thanks to God that he had been found worthy to receive such a present from the land of the English, and, said he, 'I knew indeed before, that this was the true celebration of Easter, but now I so fully know the reason for observing of this time, that I seem convinced that I knew little of it before. Therefore I publicly declare and protest to you that are here present, that I will for ever continually observe this time of Easter, with all my nation; and I do decree that this tonsure, which we have heard is most reasonable, shall be received by all the clergy in my kingdom.' Accordingly he immediately performed by his regal authority what he had said. For the circles or revolutions of nineteen years were presently, by public command, sent throughout all the provinces of the Picts to be transcribed, learned and observed, the erroneous revolutions of eighty-four years being every where suppressed. All the ministers of the altar and monks had the crown shorn, and the nation thus reformed, rejoiced, as being newly put under the direction of Peter, the most blessed prince of the apostles, and secure under his protection.

Translated by the Rev. J. A. Giles (from the edition published in 1840).

1. Nechtan

Selected Chronological Index